Author: Bri Williams
Title: Behavioural Economics for Business
Subjects: Behavioural Economics, Behavioural Influence, Decision Making, Change Management

Cover design: Bri Williams
Cover design software: Canva

To my grandfather Lawrie Griffiths
in his 101st year.

"It's a funny old world."

BEHAVIOURAL ECONOMICS FOR BUSINESS

The science of getting people to take action

Bri Williams

TABLE OF CONTENTS

PART II. APPLIED BEHAVIOURAL ECONOMICS

Chapter 13. Strategies & Positioning

Chapter 14. Innovation

Chapter 15. Final thoughts .

PART III. RESOURCES AND REFERENCES

Part I.
Business is about changing behaviour

Chapter 1. The Missing Piece

Prologue

Sitting behind the one-way glass, the team listened intently as our focus group described what would encourage them to use the printed phone book more.

"A schedule of bin days would be great", said one participant. "You know, a ready reference that I could flick to and work out which week was green waste and which was recycling?"

As a product manager for one of Australia's leading brands I was no stranger to research. Our industry was under pressure as behaviour related to searching for contact information shifted from printed phone directories to digital, and more specifically, to Google.

And like so many businesses, we sought to find answers by asking our customers. After all, who better to help co-create a service than those for whom it exists?

Welcome to *Behavioural Economics for Business*, your guide to understanding why relying on what customers tell you will doom your business to fail, and what to do instead.

Business is about changing behaviour

No matter what business you are in and what role you have, your job is to change behaviour. While for the purposes of this book I will refer to all constituent groups collectively as 'customers', you might need to change the behaviour of:

* Customers – getting them to buy, click, call, sign or pay
* Consumers – having them consume your product rather than a competitor's, refer others to you
* Suppliers – influencing them to prioritise your needs, supply on time, offer a discount
* Staff – getting them to perform, turn up, take leave, stay, go
* Investors – convincing them to support you, inject resources, be your advocate
* Stakeholders – getting them to buy-in to your plans, allocate resources to you

Whether you operate in a Business-to-Business, Business-to-Consumer or Person-to-Person context, knowing how to influence behavior – someone else's or even your own – is central to being both more effective and efficient in your endeavours because, at the end of the day, business is about changing behaviour.

Where we've gone wrong

It turns out that we've built our businesses for a type of decision-maker that doesn't exist. We've been frustrating our own efforts to get people to take action by relying on three mistaken assumptions about how behaviour is influenced.

Mistake #1: Assuming people do what they say

It was getting to the pointy end. The new non-alcoholic drink was almost ready to hit the restaurant and bar market, but a big decision was still to be made. In which colour bottle should the drink be packaged, green or amber?

Focus groups were adamant. The colour that best matched the healthy positioning of the drink was green. Words like "fresh" and "clean" were enthusiastically thrown around. But packaging experts Vivian Zurlo and Candice Dunn(1) weren't so sure.

Ask Australians whether they support Australian Made products and you'll get a passionate and patriotic response. I'm one of them. Of course I support "Australian Made"!

But watch these same Australians in the supermarket aisle as we hover around the tinned tomatoes, reaching for the Italian import on special for 99 cents. "It's OK, I'll buy Australian Made next time", we tell ourselves.

It is this gap between intended and actual behaviour that is the heart of wasted money and resources in business. Customers tell us one thing only to do another.

Like a schedule of bin days.

Focus group participants told me that it would be useful to have a schedule of bin days in their phone directory. A perfectly logical suggestion, this was attractive to me as a product manager because it meant that the phone book would be more likely to sit in an easy to access spot in the home and provide even greater utility for our customers.

Only one problem.

What do you do when you need to know which bin to put out for collection? Like most you probably walk out of your driveway to see what your neighbours have done.

And that's what packaging experts Zurlo and Dunn intuited when they heard research participants opting for the green bottle. In the hypothetical world of focus group research, people were imagining their consumption of a non-alcoholic drink and quite rationally, articulating reasons for their preference for green. But is that what they would buy?

Welcome to what I call the "Say vs. Do" gap.

The Say vs. Do gap is where we say we'll do one thing but actually do another. Things like:

* 60% of US voters claim they'll turn out to vote but only 40% do[2]

* 50% of Victorians say they eat healthily but only 7% eat their veggies[3]

* Americans claim they love Guinness but actually buy Bud Light[4]

In fairness, no one is being deliberately misleading; it's just the nature of how we behave.

When asked to explain why we've done or will do something, like in a research group, we come up with a plausible story that connects the behaviour to the rationale. "I will look up bin dates in the phone book because it makes sense for me to do that", and "I'd prefer a green bottle because that signals health". But when we are actually faced with the situation, chances are our behaviour will be shaped by how we feel in the moment, where we are, who is around and our habits.

We're going to dig a little deeper into why the Say vs. Do gap exists in Chapter 3 where you'll be introduced to **Dual Process Theory** and learn what elephants have to do with changing customer behaviour.

For now know that building your business around what customers tell you they want is setting yourself up for failure, and we need to find smarter ways of influencing customers to take action.

Glad I'm not GLAD

Leading brands are not immune to the Say vs. Do gap. In fact it's those with big research dollars that can most often fall into the trap.

In defending their decision to launch a 'new and improved' cling wrap box, GLAD's spokesperson cited extensive and positive customer research[5].

"Before making these changes [to the way the cling wrap could be cut], GLAD completed rigorous and extensive in-home research in Australia. The results were overwhelmingly positive favouring the changes including the movement of the cutter bar to the lid, with the safety aspect of this front of mind. In fact, more than 60% of those Australians, who participated in the research, preferred the improved product overall."

But when the product hit the shelves, customers hit social media to vent their outrage. GLAD quickly recanted on their decision, reverting to their old box. An expensive mistake and lesson in the perils of the "Say vs. Do" gap.

Mistake #2: Assuming people are rational

The Australian Government is one of the most progressive in anti-smoking policy. One of their Quitline online advertisements lays out a pretty grim message. The first of three panels shows the face of a grey-skinned man looking to camera like he is in a police line up. To the left of his face are listed the symptoms of quitting; headache and increased appetite. To the right, the symptoms of smoking; stroke and mouth cancer.

"A little suffering now saves a whole lot of suffering later" flashes across the second panel before panel three concludes the ad with "Stop before the real suffering starts", with a phone number to call.

This is what I call a rational message. Rationally, short-term disadvantages like increased appetite and headaches are clearly much less dire than the longer-term risks of stomach and mouth cancer. But when has it ever been a rational decision to smoke?

The trick with behaviour is that *rational doesn't always mean effective*.

In this case, what if I don't want a headache because I have a big meeting tomorrow, or an increased appetite because I want to fit into an outfit for a wedding coming up? Sure, I might face consequences down the track, but I'm concerned about just getting through the day right now.

And that can be the problem with rational messages; they overlook the unconscious factors that influence behaviour and mean we don't always do what's rationally best.

Throughout this book you will be introduced to a great many exceptions to rationality (our 'non-rationality'), starting with the reason the effectiveness of the anti-smoking ad is in doubt: our desire to act for now rather than later.

Short-term Bias

Immediate concerns usually trump those for the longer term thanks to our **Short-term Bias**. For instance, while rationally I know that stomach cancer is worse than a headache, it doesn't mean I am willing to have a sore head when I have a big meeting at work tomorrow. While rationally I understand the importance of superannuation, my immediate financial priority might be keeping my savings in an on-call account in case unexpected bills arise.

Short-term Bias means that a case that stacks up on paper can fail to persuade simply as a function of timing. If your customer has to wait for the good stuff but cop the bad stuff upfront, then you are going to struggle to convince them to take action. (More on this in Chapter 3.)

Ego Depletion

Imagine you are up for parole. Your lawyers are confident you'll be granted release after serving your time, and you've just found out that yours is the final case before the court breaks for lunch. Your cellmate is also due to be heard but has to wait until after lunch.

I have some bad news for you. All things being equal your post-lunch cellmate has a 65% chance of being granted parole whereas your last-case-before-lunch odds have dipped to a mere 10%.

At least this was what researchers studying over 1,100 parole judgements found(6). Same judges, different time of day, different result.

Turns out that the most learned judges who are trained to focus on facts and rationality are fallible humans after all. Fatigue changed their decision-making ability. Not facts. Not merit. Fatigue.

As the judges inadvertently demonstrated, once our capacity for self-control is exhausted (i.e. **Ego Depletion,** where our self-controlling Ego is spent) we tend to rely on the easiest course – either leaving things as they are (like leaving people in jail) or acting on impulse (reaching for a sugary treat after a hard day).

Throws up some questions around time of day for meetings, doesn't it?

Processing Fluency

Here's an exercise for you. Read the following and estimate, in minutes and seconds, how long you think the exercise will take to complete.

> Tuck your chin into your chest, and then lift your chin upward as far as possible. 6-10 repetitions. Lower your left ear toward your left shoulder and then your right ear toward your right shoulder. 6-10 repetitions.

Now let's do it again. How long do you think the exercise will take to complete in this case?

Tuck your chin into your chest, and then lift your chin upward as far as possible. 6-10 repetitions. Lower your left ear toward your left shoulder and then your right ear toward your right shoulder. 6-10 repetitions.

Easy? Well, probably easier in the first example than the second, right? As you may have noticed, the instructions were the same except for the typeface, and it turns out that that matters. A great deal in fact.

Researchers[7] were interested in how the ease with which we process information impacts our likelihood of embarking on the activity[8]. Using the same instructions as I've noted above, they found that those who read instructions in the easy-to-read Arial 12 Point font thought the exercise would take only 8.2 minutes, whereas those with the eye squinting, awkwardly cursive Brush Script thought it would take a whopping 15.1 minutes.

I've run this experiment in workshops where people have estimated the exercise routine in Brush Script will take up to twice as long.

Known as "**Processing Fluency**", when something is easy to read and understand we think it will require less effort to undertake.

In business that means your choice of typeface and design will have a bearing on customer perceptions of ease.

Mistake #3: Underestimating our environment

You've just walked into a room, been handed a bowl and spoon and been invited to serve yourself as much ice-cream as you want. While it might seem like heaven, this was actually the scenario faced by a lucky group of research participants.

The researchers(9) were interested in whether giving people a bigger bowl or bigger spoon impacted the amount of ice cream consumed. And sure enough, those with a randomly allocated larger rather than smaller bowl consumed 31% more ice-cream. Larger spoon? 14% more(10).

Similarly, researchers(11) were interested in whether background music would influence consumer behaviour, turning their local bottle shop into a laboratory. If you went into the bottle shop one day, French music was playing in the background, and the next day, German music. Accordion and oom-pah music rotated for a period of two weeks during which time sales of wine were monitored. The finding? Yes, music did have an impact on which wine was purchased.

When French music was played, 77% of wine purchased was French. German music? 73% of wine purchased was German.

When customers were asked about the music 86% said it did not have any effect on their decision.

Watch where you sit
Where we sit can influence our behaviour.
In an office for example, arranging chairs in circular formation cues our need for belonging and consensus whereas an angular formation does the opposite[12].

And in a restaurant, we are likely to eat more dessert if we sit in a booth but more salad if we sit by the window[13]!

It seems that we **underestimate how much the environment** impacts our behaviour.

This brings us back to the question of which bottle would be best for the non-alcoholic drink we read about earlier. You might recall that focus group participants voted for the green bottle but the specialists responsible for the decision weren't convinced.

So like any responsible marketers, they took it to the pub.

Creating product samples in both green and amber bottles, the team this time observed what participants did rather than asking them. And this time, in a real-life rather than focus group environment, the amber bottle was preferred.

The environment had flipped the result. According to Zurlo and Dunn, the amber bottle allowed people to purchase a non-alcoholic drink that looked like a regular beer, avoiding social stigma. Only by testing the product in a real-life circumstance were environmental influences like **Social Norms** observed.

Where do the three flawed assumptions about how customers behave leave us? If customers:

* don't do what they say,

* are not always rational and

* are affected by their environment

it means we've been trying to influence behaviour in the wrong way, for a type of decision maker that doesn't exist.

To borrow behavioural economist Richard Thaler's Star Trek metaphor, we've assumed we're dealing with clinical, rational, unfeeling Spock when impulsive, emotional and flawed Captain Kirk is actually the one guiding the ship(14). No wonder getting people to take action seems difficult.

Infobesity leaves us starved of answers

If yours is like most businesses, I doubt you are short on data about your customers. In fact, you might be drowning in segmentation, customer satisfaction surveys, click data, social media stats, scan data and market research. But while there may be plenty of data, that doesn't mean you are getting the answers you need.

Answers about how people will respond to something you do.

That was one of my biggest frustrations as a product manager – lots of data but no answers as to what would happen if I did something in the market.

Isn't that what we want to know? If I do this, what will my customers do?

> **The era of "Infobesity"**
> Businesses are fed a diet of quick-fix data that leaves us starved of answers and craving our next analytical hit.

We know that the Say vs. Do gap, non-rationality and hidden impact of our environment mean we can't rely on asking our customers.

So if we can't rely on self-reports, how do we get answers?

How do we *predict* what our customers will do?

Predicting Behaviour

Our ability to predict behaviour has been frustratingly elusive. We've had to gamble on what customers have told us and make assumptions based on what they have done historically.   But if we really want to drive efficiencies in our business and be much more effective, we need to base our decisions on two dimensions. Behaviour that is;
  * real not reported and
  * oriented to the future not past.

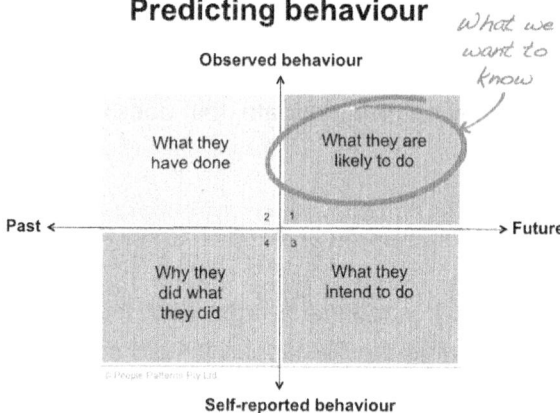

Predicting behaviour

Observed vs. Self-reported Behaviour

A significant difference between behavioural economists and other social researchers is how they seek answers. Rather than asking people, Behavioural Economists set up experiments and observe what people do.

In this way they get closer to real rather than reasoned or rationalised behaviour.

From such experiments behavioural principles are extracted to explain behavioural tendencies. The **Paradox of Choice**, where we love the freedom to choose but get overwhelmed by it, is one such example.

Future vs. Past Behaviour

It's often said that the past is the best predictor of future behaviour. Indeed the field of behavioural interviewing is predicated on that assumption – if someone has done something before they will do it again.

To a degree this has merit; habits play a large role in behaviour and if I've done something routinely I may be more likely to do that in future.

But think about your behaviour from five years ago. Are you eating the same breakfast? The same dinner? Are you in the same job? Relationship? House?

Behaviour changes and it can be dangerous to extrapolate past trends to future. Taxi companies around the world might have felt comfortable assuming past behaviour would continue, until Uber completely disrupted their business model.

So how do we get answers on what customers will do in the future without failing into the trap of self-reported intention?

Predictive analytics is an option; crunching myriad data points to build a model of expected behaviour. Retailer Target in the US famously felt the wrath of a father whose daughter had been targeted for pregnancy-related brochures, only for her to later confess that Target were right(15).

But we're talking about pretty sophisticated models here, and from my experience in the corporate sector, the promise of Big Data is still a long way from being delivered. It seems most established businesses are still grappling with legacy systems and getting the basics right rather than predicting what their customers will do.

Aside from the significant cost that puts predictive analytics beyond the reach of most small and medium businesses, the other issue is its inflexibility. Even if you get your data into a form that allows you to model the future, its validity is related to the assumptions you've used for the issue at hand. What about variants that crop up and need a fast response?

Further, predictive analytics won't help you determine how to frame an offer to that audience. Should you use this word or that in your copywriting? Where should your Call to Action be positioned and what images will be most effective?

We need, therefore, a way to help us understand and influence customers that is based on real behaviour, future oriented, inexpensive, scalable and flexible. Does such a thing exist?

The role of Behavioural Economics

Treasure maps have long held allure. The promise of riches to be gained by following a marked trail is a pretty attractive deal, and one that I make here. By understanding and applying the principles of Behavioural Economics you will be able to better influence desired outcomes. You'll have your very own behavioural treasure map.

We can create this predictive framework by using the principles of Behavioural Economics as baseline assumptions about what people will do.

For example, thanks to the principle of **Social Norms** we know that people are influenced by what others do. This means we can assess, anticipate and design the social context in which the behavioural decision may take place. By normalising the desired behaviour, we can maximise the chances our customers will follow suit.

Predicting behaviour

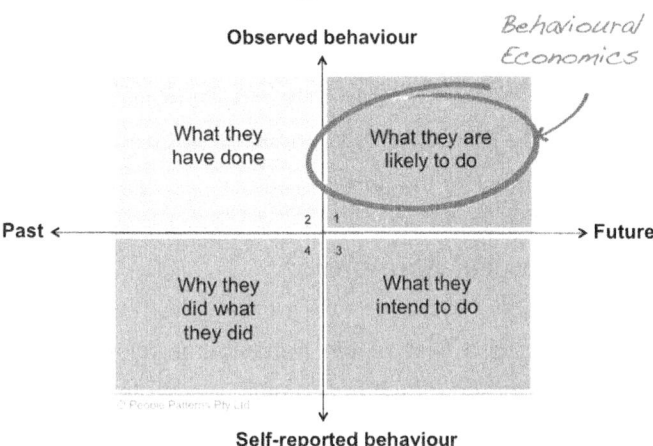

This is why Behavioural Economics can fill a gap in knowledge about human behaviour that no other data or research has been able to. It is based on observed rather than self-reported data, and can be used to anticipate future behaviour.

Behavioural Economics defined

Behavioural Economics is the study of social, cognitive and emotional *biases* and *heuristics* that influence economic decision-making behaviour.

Or put more simply, the study of why we behave the way we do(16).

Biases are hard-wired decision-making tendencies. Our Short-Term Bias means we are more interested in short-term benefits than those in the long-term, for example.

Heuristics are rules of thumb we use to make fast decisions. For instance we might use price as a signal for quality, or value brands we recognise over those we don't.

The central tenets of Behavioural Economics are that we (our customers and ourselves included):

 * don't always act in our own best interests, as judged in rational economic terms

 * are efficient rather than necessarily effective decision-makers

 * are **satisficers** more than optimisers, making 'good-enough' rather than perfect decisions most of the time

The rise of Behavioural Economics

Behavioural Economics is a field of the behavioural sciences that arose through psychologists and economists examining exceptions to traditional economic theory*(17)*. Trailblazers Daniel Kahneman, Amos Tversky and Richard Thaler began documenting evidence of rational-man going rogue, gradually building the case that people do not, in fact, always behave in ways that maximise their outcomes.

But it wasn't until around 2003 when the books Nudge and Predictably Irrational captured public attention that Behavioural Economics started to gain broader traction. Since then Thinking Fast and Slow and Misbehaving have also become New York Times bestsellers*(18)*.

One of the criticisms of the fledgling field is that Behavioural Economics is simply a re-branding of psychology*(19)*. To that I say, who cares? Anything that brings renewed excitement about a field that sheds light on human behaviour is a good thing. Behavioural Economics is being talked about in the C-Suite, highest echelons of government and around boardroom tables and that is significant progress, particularly for those who have been seeking a better way to understand and influence behaviour.

Behavioural Economics in the real world

Behavioural Economics has at last graduated from the halls of academia and is being used in fields including Technology, Healthcare, Finance, Transport, Utilities, Policy, Retail, Advertising, Education and Manufacturing.

Some examples that have been published in the public domain include:

Lloyds and Barclays banks
With the guidance of Procter research, the bank call centres were behaviourally tweaked through scripting and call pathways and reported an increase in sales of 20%, 7% improvement in satisfaction, conversion growth of almost 12% and a nearly 18% increase in staff confidence[20].

Westpac NZ
Used the behavioural insight that we spend on impulse to create a new mobile app that allows their customers to save on impulse too[21].

IKEA
It's always an adventure to shop in this monolithic furniture retailer. The stores enfold customers in an environment in which everything is perceived as low-cost, weakening their ability and motivation to compare competitive options[22].

Domino's Pizza
Is a 2-for-1 offer better at driving behaviour than a free bottle of soft drink? Domino's in the UK engaged their media agency to use Behavioural Economics in the planning process to optimise customer incentives[23].

Birmingham Airport
An airport website was turned from a cost centre to profit centre by simplifying the decision-making process for customers. As a result, traffic and conversion for parking, travel and newsletter sign-ups were all impressively improved[24].

US Cellular
Holes punched in the wall of an outlet by an angry customer triggered an overhaul of US Cellular's customer loyalty program using Behavioural Economics*(26)*.

Amp Financial Advisors
Teamed with Dan Ariely of Duke University to develop Amp's app for financial advisors, using Behavioural Economics in its design to gain an average 76% conversion*(27)*.

And these are only the cases that hit the news. For every business that spruiks its application of behavioural techniques, you can be sure there are a dozen that are keeping it quiet for competitive reasons.

Return On Investment (ROI) of Behavioural Economics

What most appeals to me about the application of Behavioural Economics to everyday business issues is this – it's free. Sure there might be some costs in getting well versed in the principles (this book, for instance), but you don't have to buy a new widget or restructure your business to gain the benefits. In fact, you can save money while increasing your effectiveness.

Let's take a look at a typical sales and marketing mix. You might invest in Above the Line (ATL) marketing like TV and radio, Digital and Social Media like your website and Facebook, Direct Marketing like printed flyers, and employing a Sales team – usually the most expensive investment of all.

Behavioural Economics ROI
Higher conversion without additional cost

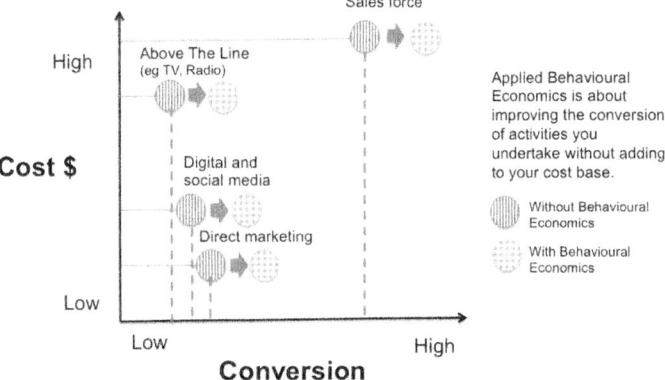

Such costs are effectively sunk – you wear them as a standard function of going to market, so imagine the upside if you could increase their effectiveness without having to spend any more? No bigger media placements. No additional sales heads. No expensive PR campaigns.

By applying behavioural science to these activities you can maximise your return on investment (ROI). This is about making small, science-based tweaks to optimise your effectiveness.

As one of my clients noted "...the number of people signing up for my newsletters has doubled while my conversion rate has increased by half over again(28)."

BE is about optimising outcomes
Behavioural Economics gives you a way to increase your effectiveness without having to spend more. It's about optimising what you were going to do anyway.

What's been holding Behavioural Economics back?

If Behavioural Economics promises such a great Return On Investment (ROI) why isn't everyone using it yet?

No one likes being called irrational

No one likes being called stupid, and no one likes being called irrational. Indeed whenever I describe behaviour as irrational in a seminar I notice crossed arms and furrowed brows.

"Sure, other people might do stupid things, but that's not me" seems to be the shared sentiment.

And it's in large part the fault of the brilliant Dan Ariely. Calling his book "Predictably Irrational" brought to the fore all the behaviour that contradicts the traditional economic theory of rational-man. Suddenly we were to think of ourselves as behaving irrationally.

But while irrationality may be correct in a definitional sense, I believe the word itself remains too strongly associated with negative connotations like stupidity to make it a comfortable moniker. "Irrational behaviour" seems to point to a flaw in personality, as if someone has taken leave of their senses.

I therefore prefer to talk about 'non-rational' behaviour, which is associated with the act of decision-making rather than the person.

Nothing new

You're a senior marketer who is in the final stages of a landmark campaign. All you need now is sign off from your CEO. The ad agency joins you as you take your boss through what the campaign's rationale and creative plans.

"Don't like it," your CEO barks. "Why not make it blue and have a dog in the ad?"

Along with Human Resources professionals, marketers have always had my sympathy. Despite most being highly qualified and experienced, those in "soft skills" roles suffer from the profession's perceived low barriers to entry. In short, anyone with an opinion thinks they are qualified to do your job.

This is why I used to think marketers would be the first to jump on Behavioural Economics as 'their' field. Where an accountant has Accounting Standards to govern and protect their profession, marketers could claim this arm of behavioural science to support their work and raise the barriers to their profession in the process.

But that's not been my observation. While many marketers have of course embraced Behavioural Economics (my clients among them) I have also noticed a reticence across pockets of the profession.

This is my hypothesis as to why. As a marketer you are being paid to know how to influence people. It can be difficult, therefore, to put your hand up and admit that there are gaps in that knowledge. It's easier to say you already know and that there's nothing new in Behavioural Economics. For reasons we've covered in the flawed assumptions section, like the Say vs. Do gap, non-rational behaviour, and the underestimated role of our environment, that's a mistake.

Lack of framework

Wrapping your arms around the sprawling and evolving field of Behavioural Economics is no simple task. While reading studies or the books examining them are helpful both in bringing to light how the principles have been identified and positing their application, how on earth do you consolidate the principles? How do you take all of what has been unearthed and bind them in a framework that you can use across day-to-day business challenges?

This, I believe, has been the fundamental reason Behavioural Economics has not yet pervaded the business community; we haven't had a meaningful framework to use.

The closest we have come to resolving this issue have sprung from the government sector, M.I.N.D.S.P.A.C.E.*(29)* and E.A.S.T.*(30)*.

While excellent mnemonics that capture the most popular principles (I have my own called I.N.F.L.U.E.N.C.E.S.*(31)*, which you can read about in Part III), I believe we can and need to go further.

To apply Behavioural Economics we need a framework that not only prompts ideas about how to solve the issue, but helps identify what type of issue we have in the first place.

That's what this book provides. In the next chapter you will be introduced to my framework for analysing and resolving any business issue that requires you to get customers to take action. A simple framework that belies the complexity of what it enables you to do, it starts by defining the core challenge confronting every business:

How to change behaviour.

Chapter 2. Defining the Core Business Challenge

Before we dive into changing customer behaviour, let's consider the approach taken to one of the trickiest, stickiest behaviours: Smoking.

"A little bit of suffering now saves a whole lot of suffering later".

You'll recall this is the key message in one of the Australian Government's anti-smoking ads. You might also recall my concern that it relies on a rational, System 2 message.

Thankfully this ad is only one part of a much larger program to reduce rates of smoking, and just as well. With smoking, along with most types of behaviour change, for too long we've assumed all we needed do was explain to people why they should change and they would. Education was seen as the answer. But here's an extract from a report on the impact of anti-smoking ad campaigns*(32)*;

> *"The data suggest that a significant proportion of the population does not heed anti-smoking health messages. In their economic modelling, Bardsley and Olekalns (1999) found that anti-smoking advertising and education had no significant effect on smoking behaviour, but that workplace smoking bans and health warnings on cigarette packs decreased consumption. They argued that the overwhelming evidence was that of various policy interventions in the 35 years to their research, taxation of tobacco products had been the most effective in reducing aggregate tobacco consumption (Bardsley & Olekalns, 1999)."*

So why persist with these campaigns? It makes it seem like you are doing something (which is perhaps one of the reasons they are so popular with government). It's hard to be criticised for giving people more information.

It's time to burst that bubble.

While an appealingly safe option, more information is typically not the answer. At least, not when you are trying to change someone's behaviour.

Rarely is inaction a result of deficient knowledge.

We know superannuation is important. That doesn't mean we do anything about it.

We know a healthy lifestyle is a function of what we eat and drink, how much we move our bodies, mindfulness and connections with those around us, yet it doesn't mean we necessarily prioritise those aspects of our life.

We know it's dangerous to exceed the speed limit, but if we're running late…

The upshot is we need to stop assuming "knowing" is the answer and instead focus our attention on "doing".

> **Knowing isn't always the answer**
> Stop assuming knowing is the answer. Focus on doing.

Let's say you are running a workshop and one of the participants, Sam is sitting in a chair to your left. How would you go about getting Sam to move from the current chair to one on the right?

You could perhaps explain why Sam should move, using education as your strategy? Or perhaps use an incentive, paying Sam to move? You could even physically move Sam, applying force. But how do you know which approach will be most effective without having to guess?

Whether it's getting someone to move chairs or influencing customer behaviour we need a way of analysing the problem so we can then design an appropriate and effective solution.

It's as simple as A, B, see?

Boil it down and everything in business revolves around getting people from point A to point B; getting them to move from what they are currently doing to what we want them to do. In this case, we are trying to get Sam to move from the current chair (A) to the new chair (B).

This is the foundation of our behavioural strategy; defining both the current and desired behaviours. Ask yourself three questions:
1. What is the context? (Where are they, who are they, when are they doing what they're doing?)
2. What are our customers currently doing? (A)
3. What do we want our customers to do? (B)

By asking these three simple questions you will get clarity on the scale of your behaviour change task.

Don't be fooled. As straightforward as these questions seem, this is where businesses usually go wrong. In our haste to get moving we tend to skip to ideas getting people to do what we want without understanding what they are doing right now.

That's a mistake. To change behaviour requires we **break a pattern of existing behaviour**, and that means we need to understand the status quo.

To get people to do something new means unshackling them from the old.

> **Example: Getting people to go to the dentist**
> A private health insurer was seeking to get members to
> visit the dentist more regularly to reduce health care
> costs.
>
> Here's how we can break down the behavioural task.
>
> We write down three statements and describe what we
> know about each.
>
> **1. When they**...(describe the context)
> e.g. When our members are living day to day during
> the year
> **2. They**...(describe current behaviour A.)
> e.g. They are failing to make time to go to the dentist
> **3. They**...(describe desired behaviour B.)
> e.g. They book and attend the dentist at least once
> every 12 months

Status Quo Bias, the nemesis of behaviour change

If there is a villain in this book it is named Status Quo Bias. Like Darth Vader to Luke Skywalker and Kryptonite to Superman, Status Quo Bias is the nemesis of behaviour change.

Status Quo is our tendency to leave things as they are.

Let's say, for example that you have to decide what to do with some stocks in your portfolio. Thanks to status quo bias we know you will be more likely stick with shares you already own rather than switch to alternatives even if they are no longer the best for you.

Further, the greater the number of options you have to consider, the more likely you are not to change. According to the researchers, "The greater the number of alternatives offered, the more pronounced the Status Quo Bias is. The Status Quo Bias if there are more than 100 alternatives is three times as large as if there are only less than 25 alternatives*(33)*."

It's interesting that more choice can result in less choosing. But like any good villain, Status Quo is not all bad. There are times when this inertia can work in our favour. Sometimes we want customers to leave things as they are: price rises and retention for instance.

But if your objective is to get your customer to do something new or different we need to think of the challenge as one of breaking status quo.

Approaching the situation in this way forces you to get into the customer's mind-set. You'll have to think about what they have to give up in order to move in the direction you want, and rather than simply focussing on the benefits of the change, you will shift your attention to its potential downsides – the things that are getting in the way of your customer taking action. What you have to do to overcome these barriers will become clear.

A Model for Behaviour Change

Now that you have spent time identifying the context, the current and the desired behaviours it's time to understand how we break status quo and get customers from A to B.

Unfortunately there is no direct path between these points, which is why we waste significant effort and resources on sales, marketing and leadership programs that don't achieve their objectives. Instead we have to zig before we can zag. Behavioural Economics is what we'll be using to guide us, analysing what prevents our customers from taking action, and helping us to devise solutions to compel them.

Three barriers to taking action

There are three central behavioural barriers to behaviour that stand in the way of you influencing your customer to take action:

1. Apathy – your customer simply can't be bothered intellectually, emotionally or physically to do what you want

2. Paralysis – your customer is overwhelmed by the decision

3. Anxiety – your customer is worried about proceeding

These form the left hand side of the Williams Behaviour Change Model below. We'll be using this model to navigate our way from A to B.

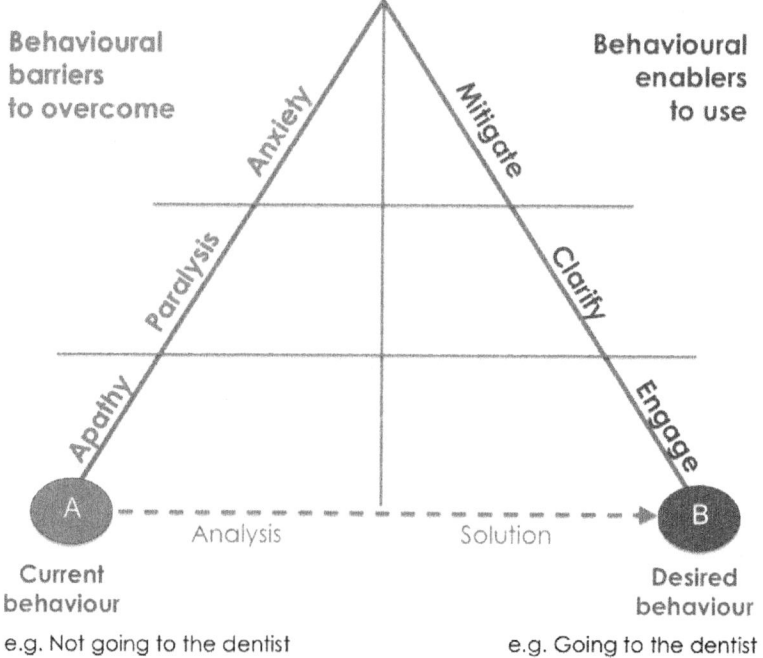

Williams Behaviour Change Model

We can use the Behaviour Change Model to analyse a range of behaviour change challenges. For instance, if getting Sam to move chairs in our challenge, barriers may include Sam being:

* too lazy to move (Apathy)

* happy with their current chair and position (Apathy)

* confused about which chair to move to (Paralysis)

* worried about the attention they're receiving and feeling embarrassed to move (Anxiety)

* worried about being separated from their friends (Anxiety)

Another example. The private health insurer might struggle to get their members to attend the dentist annually because they:

* find going to the dentist boring and feel they have better things to do (Apathy)

* can't decide which dentist to go to, so end up not going to any (Paralysis)

* are worried about the cost or pain of going to the dentist (Anxiety)

Or how about a superannuation fund that wants to get people to increase their contributions? Barriers may include:

* finding superannuation boring and customers feeling they have better things to do than fill in forms (Apathy)

* the inability to decide between investment options, instead preferring to leave things as they were originally set up (Paralysis)

* fear that paying money into super means they might get caught short if an unexpected expense crops up (Anxiety)

Use of the model across industry and business size

The Behaviour Change Model is:

* flexible; able to be applied across all industries and organisations of any size, and

* scalable; helping you unblock large scale, macro behavioural challenges (e.g. how to get people to go to the dentist) along with micro tasks (e.g. getting people to complete a form.

In the chapters that follow you will become very familiar with the three barriers to change - Apathy, Paralysis and Anxiety - as well as how each barrier may be addressed.

> ## A model for any challenge, anywhere
>
> ### Industry agnostic
> The Williams Behaviour Change Model has been applied across industries as diverse as banking, superannuation, pest control, financial planning, weight management, health and life insurance, retail and advertising; for small and medium businesses and large corporations; and across private, public and not-for-profit sectors.
>
> ### Scalable, from macro to micro
> The model is scalable and can resolve both macro (e.g. how to get people to act on their superannuation) and micro (e.g. how do we get people to click that button) issues.

It's worth noting before we get stuck into the detail of the model that the order of barriers is not fixed. While Apathy appears first in the model, by no means is it a precursor or more/less important than the other two. In some cases you may find all three barriers at work, in others, only one. Even if it turns out that one barrier isn't at play, the important thing is you have asked the question.

With that in mind let's now dive in to Apathy: how to get your customer to be bothered.

Chapter 3. Apathy

"Scientists found a cure for apathy, but no one seemed to care"

Roadblock number one on our road to changing behaviour is Apathy.

As frustrating as talking to a wall, Apathy describes the situation in which your customer is simply uninterested in whatever you are suggesting; they are too cognitively lazy to be bothered. They're thinking "I have zero interest in what you are saying."

Before spending more time and money trying to convince them to do business with you, let's get to the bottom of why people tune out. It starts by thinking of your customers as having two heads.

Dual Process Theory

Dual Process Theory describes how we switch between conscious and unconscious thinking throughout the day. In a sense it's like having two heads.

Psychologist and one of the founding fathers of Behavioural Economics Daniel Kahneman differentiates these two systems by whether intuition or reasoning is engaged and describes them as System 1 and System 2(34),.

System 1 is our default, and was the first type of thinking we developed (hence being number 1). Instinctual, fast, habitual, emotional and efficient, System 1 is the part of us that drives the car to a familiar place without needing to concentrate.

With massive processing capacity – the equivalent to over 11,000,000 bits of data per second, System 1 dominates everyday decision-making(35).

System 2 is a higher-order type of thinking that is more cognitively taxing. Slow, rational, detail-oriented and precise, System 2 is the part of us that takes charge of the car when we are driving somewhere less familiar or in dangerous conditions. System 2 responds to facts, logic and detail.

With processing capacity of a mere 40-50 bits per second, System 2 is exhaustible and therefore called upon only when the situation demands. It's our mind's equivalent of "In Case of Emergency, Break Glass".

Importantly neither system is better than the other. Both play their role and have strengths and weaknesses.

Where System 1 saves us a lot of energy by automating and fast-tracking decisions, it can sometimes lead to sub-optimal choices like buying on impulse, acting on habit or over indulging.

System 2 tends to make more considered decisions but drains our mental batteries. Once depleted, System 2 goes off duty and leaves us open to System 1 impulsiveness (which is why, exhausted by the rigours of the week pizza and beer on the Friday seem like a good idea).

In business dual processing creates problems in two ways.

First, when we ask a customer what they want we typically get an answer from System 2 - the part that deals with unusual and important situations. The problem is System 1 – the home of habits – is the one likely to be calling the shots in the real world. This is why we have the 'Say vs. Do' gap; System 2 says, System 1 does.

Second, when trying to influence customer behaviour we tend to pitch System 2 facts, figures and logic to System 1. The result? Apathy. Customers don't care because we've been pitching the wrong kind of argument.

Elephant and Rider

Another way to wrap your head around Dual Process Theory is to think of an elephant. Sitting atop this massive beast is a person; let's call them the Rider(36).

While the Rider has the reins and pretends to be in charge, the sheer difference in mass means the Elephant doesn't go anywhere it doesn't want to go. The Rider may think they're in charge, but it's more a case of changing their plans to accommodate the Elephant's wishes.

The Elephant represents System 1 and the Rider, System 2. Remember, System 1 (the Elephant) can process 11,000,000 bits of data per second and System 2 (the Rider), only 40-50.

The truth is the Elephant – our non-rational System 1 which is the home of habit, intuition and fast-thinking – runs the show.

The Rider – our rational System 2 – is left to post-rationalise what the Elephant has done. "Of course I meant to sleep through my alarm. Getting up early on a Monday for a run would mean I would be tired for my big meeting in the afternoon. I'll go for a run later in the week."

> **Who's in charge of the alarm clock?**
> Imagine it's Sunday night and you have decided to get up early on Monday and go for a run. System 2 is the part of you that sets the intention – and the alarm.
>
> System 1 (the Elephant) is the part of you that slaps the snooze button in the morning before you are even fully awake.
>
> To make sense of it all System 2 (the Rider) then rationalises reasons it wasn't a good idea to get up early anyway!

How businesses fail to address Apathy

When you fail to engage your customer, Apathy is the response and inaction the result. Typically the failure to engage arises from six mistakes businesses make.

1. Effort vs. Reward

Ultimately the challenge of influencing behaviour can be summed up by what I call the "**Effort vs. Reward**" equation.
* When Effort is greater than Reward, behaviour change doesn't happen
* When Reward is greater than Effort, behaviour change does happen

Where **Reward** is the payoff your customer receives (things like peace of mind, convenience or status), **Effort** can include;

* **Psychological effort** – what my colleagues or friends will think about my decision, how anxious I feel about what you are asking me to do, how smart or stupid I feel trying to do what you are asking.

* **Physical effort** – how far my eyes have to travel across the page, how easy or difficult the fonts are to read, how many clicks I have to go through, how much data entry is required, how far away your business is

* **Economic effort** – what it costs me in time and money

The Effort vs. Reward equation

© People Patterns Pty Ltd

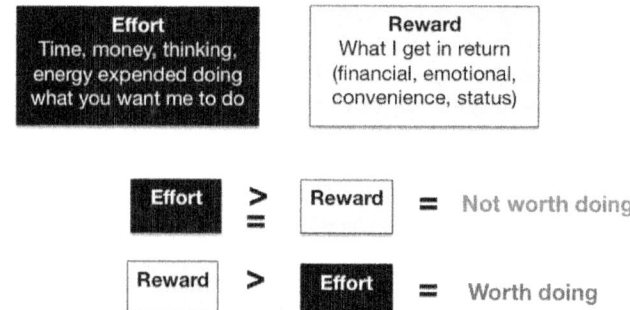

Effort	Reward
Time, money, thinking, energy expended doing what you want me to do	What I get in return (financial, emotional, convenience, status)

Effort $\geq$ Reward = Not worth doing

Reward > Effort = Worth doing

As business people we are usually great at focussing on the Reward side of the equation – what customers get – but often neglect the Effort we are asking of them. That's how we end up with websites that ask a lot but give very little.

Example of Effort exceeding Reward

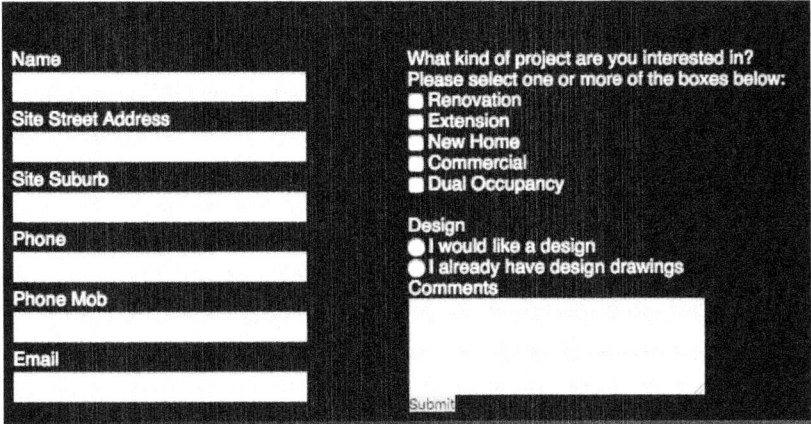

This enquiry form on a builder's website makes a number of errors.

Too hard to read

The design choice of white typeface in small font on a black background makes it difficult to read. This creates **"disfluency"** which means the state of 'flow' has been interrupted, pushing the customer out of the System 1 fast-thinking and into cranky, critical, detail oriented System 2.

Too much to do

The site confronts the prospective customer with nine fields of information to complete in order to submit their enquiry That's a lot of effort for very little reward.

Too many distractions

The enquiry form was placed on a congested page wihich included social media buttons (e.g. Twitter, Facebook). Unfortunately these icons seemed more interesting than the form, distracting customers and leading them away from contacting the business.

Unclear Call to Action

The site also squashed the "submit" button Call to Action at the bottom of the form which could easily be missed (more on Call to Action design in Chapter 9).

Reward has to exceed effort

The trick when it comes to Effort vs. Reward is that it's not enough for these two factors to be in balance. Such is the pull of status quo that to get someone to take action we need Reward to exceed Effort.

This is due to what's called **Loss Aversion** which we explore in greater detail in Chapter 5. For now it's enough to know that getting someone to do something means they have to give something else up – time, money, effort - and that means your reward has to be worthwhile.

2. Wrong thing stands out

What attracts your attention when you glance at this website?

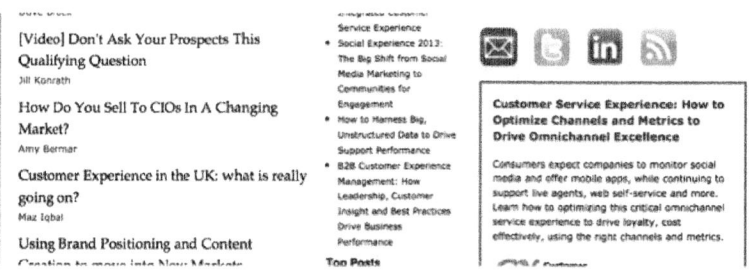

I bet it's the social media icons, right? Our attention can't help but be lured to the buttons as they most colourful elements on the page, drawing us away from the core content.

This is a case of the **wrong thing standing out,** which means the customer's System 1 will be attracted to things that are unusual, fun or salient. They can't be bothered to pay attention to what "should be" their focus.

As a business you therefore have to be very careful about how you engage the lazy brain of your customer. Here's how one manufacturer is using System 1 to advantage.

"Up to 100% softer in 1 wash" claims the shampoo. "Great!", thinks System 1 as you place the bottle in your cart, before System 2 has woken up to the fact that that could mean only 1% softer.

But not all marketers get it right. You may have heard of a washing detergent called "Black Wash" which is used to retain the colour in dark clothes. Imagine that you are looking for Black Wash in the supermarket. Up and down the aisle you go, looking for Black Wash, Black Wash, Black Wash. Hmmm seems they don't stock it. Better luck next time.

Actually they did stock Black Wash – right there in the RED bottle! Red?!

In this case the manufacturer has missed the opportunity to engage System 1, habitual thinking because they've used packaging that is disfluent with the product. While red may stand out for some products, it doesn't support a product called Black Wash. The manufacturer is relying on customer willingness to expend System 2 effort in their search, and reducing their odds of securing the sale as a result.

3. Nothing stands out

As proud business owners and leaders we too often fall into the trap of believing everything is equally important to our customers. The downside is it doesn't help customers know what is most important. The result is websites like this:

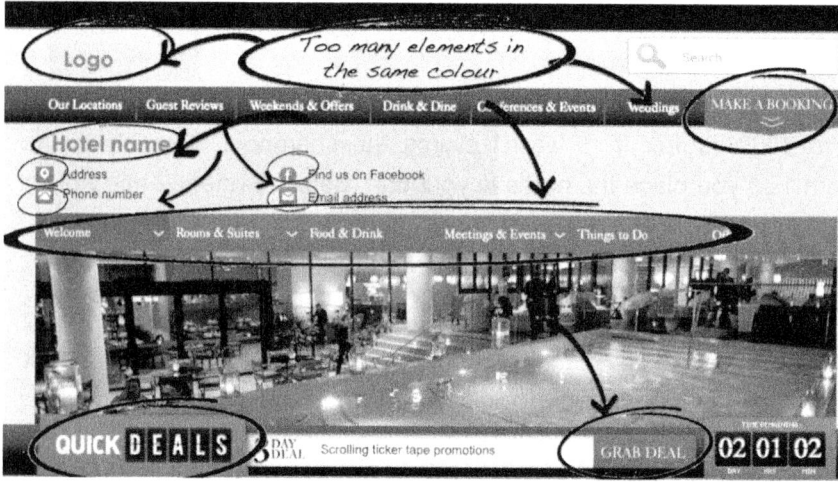

Notice how it's difficult to work out what the most important first step is? By making all the Call to Action (CTA) buttons – make a booking, address, phone number, Facebook, email and Grab a Deal - the same colour as each other and their branding (in this case red) the business is weighting the importance of each element equally.

The result is they are effectively shouting "look at me! No, look at me! Over here, it's me you should look at!", leaving the customer confused as to what they should do. As soon as the Effort to take action is greater than any Reward from doing so the customer will leave.

4. Don't see value

Call it a sign of the times, but "What's in it for me?" (WIIFM) looms large in the mind of your customer. We need to articulate why our suggestion is great value and worth bothering about.

Sadly we can often overlook this, neglecting to tell the customer why it's worthwhile. Here's a typical newsletter sign up request, for instance. The good news is they have limited the effort to only two fields. The bad news is they haven't explained the reward – what's in it for me if I give you my email?

SIGN UP TO OUR NEWSLETTER

Get the Latest from

Name *

Email *

Postcode *

Sign Up

Here's another example, this time from an accounting firm who send letters of engagement to prospective clients.

Fees

Our estimated fee for the completion of work as per the appendix A scope of services will be up to $2,000 plus GST.

If we identify any matters outside the above scope that we believe should be addressed to achieve the most beneficial outcome for you, we will contact you first to confirm your instructions. We will discuss the likely fees associated with this work at that time.

The fee for the engagement is clearly articulated, the benefits are not. How can I know if $2,000 is great value? Always remember that price is a very tangible representation of Effort for your customer – they have to pay, after all - and therefore should always be accompanied by a reminder of the Reward they can expect to receive.

5. No immediate benefit

We've already met Short-term Bias (which is also known as **Hyperbolic Discounting** and **Present-term Bias**) which is our tendency to be drawn toward things that give us pleasure in the short-term, while delaying things with a cost until later. In business this means our customers will be concerned with what they can get now, and what they can leave till later. Propositions without an immediate benefit will therefore struggle to influence action.

A helpful way of thinking about your customer's mind set is to use two time horizons: **Now Me** and **Future Me***(37)*.

"Now Me" is governed by how your customer feels in the moment. "Future Me" is a version of themselves that they push things on to, guessing that they will be better able to deal with them at a future time (when they are less busy/stressed/tired or more rested/wealthy/interested).

Now Me wants to buy those shoes on sale, so Future Me can worry about her superannuation next month.

Now Me is tired and wants to sit on the couch, so Future Me will go to the gym tomorrow.

Now Me wants to eat the chocolate cake. Future Me can eat salad for the rest of the week.

When it comes to forecasting the needs of future selves, such as structuring inventory and product offerings, there are two traps we have to avoid.

Future Me is virtuous
The first is that our customers will think they'll be more virtuous tomorrow than they actually will be.

For example, if I ask you to nominate the movies you want to watch over the next month you are likely to select a range of high-brow, art-house films. By contrast, if you are making your choice of movie to watch tonight you are more likely to opt for the Adam Sandler flick (and shame on you).

That's what happened when researchers asked two different groups of people to choose movies in either a sequential (i.e. choosing as they went) or simultaneous (i.e. choosing ahead of time) condition, with people opting for the highbrow only when "Future Me" had to watch it(38).

Future Me is more virtuous than Now Me

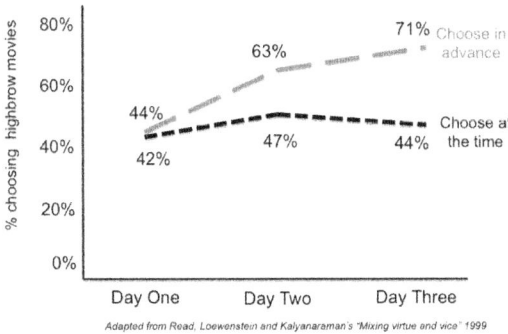

Adapted from Read, Loewenstein and Kalyanaraman's "Mixing virtue and vice" 1999

This was the same with food preferences, with researchers finding that healthier food options were selected when pre-ordered, and less healthy options consumed when the decision was made on the spot*(39)*.

Future Me wants variety

Ever come home from holiday having only worn a few of the dozen outfits you packed? This brings us to the second trap where our customers think they'll want more variety in their choices than they'll actually end up using. If, for example, I ask you to pre-order your lunches for the coming week, chances are you'll make a broader selection than if you were to make the decision about what to eat on the day.

This is known as **"Diversification Bias"** and according to researchers we overestimate our desire for different options by as much as 20%*(40)*.

Short-term Bias combined with overestimation of virtue and variety means that we not only have to deliver a sense of benefit to our customers in the immediate term, but take with a grain of salt the expectations they have about their own future needs.

6. No one else cares, why should I?

"Public apathy is more powerful than public opinion. There's more of it." Dr. Jim Boren, author of the satirical '*When in Doubt Mumble: A Bureaucrat's Handbook*" was onto something when he pointed to the power of collective behaviour, or in this case, non-behaviour.

Throughout this book you will read a lot about Social Norms, the normalised behaviour of others, because it is so influential. When in doubt we look to what people like us are doing, and in the case of Apathy, if they are doing nothing, then we will likely follow.

Take an income protection insurance ad I saw online for instance*(41)*. The ad cites two statistics. The first mentions that "96% of Australian parents with dependent children have inadequate levels of insurance cover", and the second, that "only 31% (of Australians) protect their income".

The message they are intending to convey is that Australians are neglecting their insurance and should really do something about it.

However, System 1 consumes the message in an entirely different way, along the lines that:
  * "96%? No one else is worried" and
  * "*only* 31%? Most don't bother, so why should I?"

In this way Social Norms can be a trap for unwitting businesses who inadvertently normalise rather than demonise the status quo.

> **To change behaviour**
> Don't normalise status quo. Demonise it!

We've just walked through six ways businesses fail to address Apathy:
  1. Effort exceeds Reward
  2. Wrong thing stands out
  3. Nothing stands out
  4. Don't see value
  5. No immediate benefit
  6. No one else cares, so why should I?

In each case, the Elephant is simply not engaged, and as a result, we're left with status quo. If we want to get our customers to act we therefore need strategies to get the Elephant moving, which is where we turn next.

How to overcome customer Apathy

To overcome Apathy we need to **engage** our customers. More specifically, work with their System 1 elephant thinking to persuade them to act in the way we want.

Let's look at eight behavioural strategies to get them engaged.

1. Make it easy

You'll recall that when Effort is greater than Reward behaviour doesn't happen. While it is natural to focus on the benefits of what you offer, Rewards have to be effectively double the Effort in order to bump people out of their status quo.

That means you have two levers to pull – increase the Reward (which can be very costly) or, instead of over engineering what you provide – reduce the Effort by making it easier to do business with you.

That's what Red Tomato pizza in Dubai has done(42). Select customers receive a fridge magnet that contains a computer chip loaded with their favourite pizza and payment details. Customers simply push a button on the magnet and their choice of pizza is delivered to their door. Easy? You betcha! In 4 weeks and with a budget of only $9,000, Red Tomato increased deliveries by 500% and generated over $8 million in free media.

Another example comes to us by way of the cutlery drawer(43). Managers of the staff cafeteria at the London Borough of Hounslow were getting frustrated that employees weren't returning utensils. After running an awareness campaign across the two thousand staff, and even offering a cutlery amnesty, they eventually struck on the idea of just making it easier to return the silverware. Staff can now deposit their utensils in a container provided in each break room. Easy.

The lesson from both examples is that eliminating points of friction from your process that do not add value to the customer can end up adding value to you. Make it easy.

2. Make it difficult (The Egg Theory)

At the risk of confusing things after we've just been talking about making things easy for your customer, sometimes it's even better to make it more difficult. Let me explain.

Where 'making it easy' was about eliminating points of friction that didn't add any value to the process, 'making it difficult' is a strategy to use when you need to deliberately interrupt the customer's System 1 to get them to pay attention.

Imagine you have promised yourself that you will cycle rather than drive to work but every morning you find yourself in the car before you've even remembered your promise. So engrained is your commuting habit that your System 1 auto-pilot needs to be given a severe bump to remind you to get on your bike.

Enter the clever folk at Pleasurabletroublemakers(44) who created a special key hook for just this scenario. When you grab your car keys from their hook, the hook holding the bike keys also opens, dropping them to the floor. As you stoop down to scoop up the keys you are reminded of your promise and have a chance to re-evaluate your decision to drive. By deliberately adding friction into the process – by making it difficult – they are helping their customers adhere to their desired behaviour.

The secret behind this technique is 'disfluency', and we met it briefly in Chapter 1 when exercise instructions written in one typeface were estimated to take half the time of those in a more difficult typeface. While in this case the difficult typeface worked against the objective of getting people to exercise, in some cases it can work to your advantage.

In fact a benefit of typeface that is more difficult to read is that it can force the reader to focus on detail. Research participants in one case were significantly more likely to answer a riddle correctly when the typeface was harder to read - either italicised, greyed out or condensed, because it interrupted their System 1 auto pilot and forced their System 2 to focus(45).

But that's not all. Not only does interrupting a customer's flow give them an opportunity to reset and choose their intended (non-habitual) path, making it difficult can also increase levels of commitment through having 'skin in the game'.

Take cake mix for instance. Sales of cake mix were sluggish in the 1950s until savvy marketers from Betty Crocker made the cakes more difficult to bake(46). How? They removed the dehydrated egg from the mix and instead made customers crack and whisk their own egg. Where before home cooks didn't feel they had worked sufficiently hard to present the cake as their own, they had now contributed sufficient effort to justify their baking credentials. The Egg Theory was hatched.

Commitment devices

Along with this somewhat confounding quirk where making something more difficult makes it more attractive is the surprising notion that customers may even *pay extra* for products and services that make life harder. "**Commitment devices**" are ways of ensuring we do something by locking ourselves into the consequences, and can be very attractive to customers who are struggling to stick to their goals.

Perhaps no better demonstration of this is stickK, a free goal-setting platform created by behavioural economists from Yale University(47).

Let's say my goal is to go to the gym three times a week or write 1,000 words a day for example. Using stickK I have to deposit an amount of money that will be released back to me only if I achieve my goal.

If I fail to stick to what I promised I'd do, the money is taken away, donated either to a charity I support, or, if I need even extra motivation, a charity I dislike! Central to the stickK proposition is the behavioural principle of Loss Aversion, something with which you'll become very familiar in Chapter 5. In simple terms losing hurts more than winning, and we fight harder if we have something at stake.

Supporting self-control

Many of us struggle with self-control. We might eat too much, drink too much, save too little or engage in behaviour that is not great for our health. Thankfully researchers have recently devised a strategy to help us with our self-control*(48)*.

"Temptation Bundling" is a way to overcome resistance to something we *should do* by adding it to something we *want to do*.

Here's how it works.

Say you love a TV program, like Game of Thrones, and hate exercise but know you should do it. Bundling these activities together – your 'want to do' and your 'should do' – by making a rule that you can only watch Game of Thrones at the gym, means you'll increase the likelihood of getting your 'should do' done.

Here's what the researchers who had people do just that had to say.

> *"Our research adds to a growing body of evidence that many people are aware of the limitations of their willpower and are actively seeking new avenues for overcoming those limitations".*

Sounds like fertile ground for business innovation if you ask me.

> **Effort needs to be valued**
> Making it difficult for customers has clear benefits
> when used well.
>
> But beware.
>
> The extra effort has to be valued. It has to be
> something the customer feels good about. Simply
> making it harder will create frustration and they are
> likely to take their business elsewhere.

3. Create a pain point

How do you get people to consider a product they haven't recognised a need for? In other words, how do you get your customer to be bothered to think about you?

Our third option is to create a pain point.

A clever example of doing just that comes to us via an advertisement for eye drops(49). The poster asks us to "take the 10 second dry eye test" by staring into the image without blinking.

We then read further down the poster, which informs us that if our eyes stung, burned or watered then we may have 'dry eyes'. The solution is to use their eye drops.

Now as you've probably realised, staring at any image for 10 seconds will more than likely cause them to sting, burn or water. That is, after all, what we try to avoid by blinking every 2-10 seconds.

But setting aside the ethics of their approach, I do have to commend them on how behaviourally effective the ad is. You see the ad creates a pain point, and once that is established, we're motivated to find a solution.

It doesn't just work for eye drops.

My computer was running more slowly than I wanted. In my research I came across Clean My Mac 3, a free download that diagnoses the reasons for poor speed.

Free indeed. So why do I now happily pay?

The first step ws getting me to run their diagnostic tool to identify the source of my slow performance. My points of pain became very clear and I was engaged in their product.

Then they had to make me interested enough to upgrade from a free 500MB data clean-up to the full service. To do this they showed me the remaining redundant files and offered me a click-of–the-button path to clean those too.

Both the eye drop and software businesses engaged their customer and overcame Apathy by making the pain point obvious and then following with a solution.

Using pain points to engage
- Pain points are most effective if they are delivered without judgment (don't personalise the issue or your customer will get too defensive)
- Ensure the pain point is significant from the customer's perspective, not yours
- Don't confuse a pain point with something you are doing that frustrates them!
- The solution must seem easy – don't overwhelm them with options or caveats

4. Design the environment

Your team are meeting to brainstorm some new ideas for product pipeline. Where should you hold the meeting?

Before you dive for the room that is closest or most available, consider the height of the ceiling. Researchers have discovered that higher ceilings prime people for expansive, abstract thinking whereas pokier rooms help us to focus us on detail(50).

It seems we subconsciously seek congruence between our environment and task. In the research study, for instance, participants were able to solve anagrams related to 'freedom' faster in a high-ceiling room but struggled with anagrams related to confinement. In another case, people were found to be more likely to vote in favour of funding a school initiative if they voted in a school rather than church hall(51).

Even the way chairs are set out can impact behaviour. A circular formation has been found to cue a need for belonging where people are more persuaded by others, whereas an angular formation cues uniqueness and a reduced likelihood of being persuaded by others(52).

In behavioural terms we are talking about **"priming"** - evoking a subconscious reaction that influences behaviour. In effect, you are setting the mood for the customer's brain to make decisions in your favour.

Here's just a sample of how changes in the environmental context have changed behaviour:

   * People consumed beer faster when drinking from a curved glass(53)

   * Larger popcorn boxes lead people to eat more, even though it was stale(54)!

   Inserting a "stop sign" red-coloured Pringle meant that people were cued to think about how many potato chips they were consuming, and so ate less(55)*

   * Placing ice-cream behind opaque rather than clear glass reduced consumption*(56)*

   Moving healthy food choices within easy reach and less healthy items out of direct line of sight has improved nutrition at school cafeterias(57)*

   * Presenting three options tends to result in the middle option being selected, the aptly termed "Centre-stage effect"*(58)*

Common amongst all these studies was how people were **subconsciously influenced to behave in a certain way**. It was not a matter of price, facts, information or logic.

Of course we know intuitively our environment makes a difference – why else would we bother decorating our home - but we tend to underestimate what the impact can be, particularly in a work context. It means that by making some simple changes to your business environment you might be able to improve your outcomes.

Retail performance

Retailers have long understood the power of the environment. A few examples of behaviourally effective shop design are listed below*(59)*.

JB Hi-Fi: With it's garish yellow and black "hand written" typeface point of sale and chaotic, ramshackle, bargain basement displays electronics retailer JB Hi-Fi leads customers to believe that everything is marked down. As a result, customers develop a false sense of security that they will get the cheapest price.

Apple: In keeping with their product ethos, electronics manufacturer Apple has designed stores to be clean and streamlined. They've eliminated cash registers and formal queuing and work hard to make everything seem effortless. When you visit an Apple store you feel like the burden of decision-making has been lifted and that whatever advice is offered is sound. Suddenly what you pay for solving your problem seems irrelevant.

IKEA: Furniture retailer IKEA have drummed into their market the low cost for Swedish design so when you are in-store you find adding low cost items to your cart psychologically painless. With their unique product range they have also inhibited the customer's ability to compare value of items with competitors. And they sell meatballs.

Staff performance

When it comes to the environment, don't limit your thinking to how it may influence customers. The environment impacts staff health and performance as well. For example, by redesigning its cafeteria Google has influenced its staff to consume 9% fewer lollies, 7% less soft drink and 47% more water(60). They did this by making sweet snacks and soft drinks more difficult to reach, and placing healthy options in line of sight.

> **Where you meet, matters**
> Choose your meeting location carefully, and adjust the chairs according to your objective. Look for a round table for consensus or an angular one for robust debate.

5. Mirror the body

Imagine you have three ads for yogurt in front of you. The first has a tub of yogurt with a spoon oriented to the right, the second, a tub with the spoon on the left and in the third there is no spoon. According to researchers the first ad will outperform the other two because of the **"Visual Depiction Effect**(61)**"**.

In short, we relate better to ads that depict our natural usage, so if we use a spoon in our right hand, an ad with a spoon to the right will require us to do less thinking and it will therefore seem easier. If this sounds familiar it's because it relates to Processing Fluency, the ease with which information is processed.

The importance of message orientation doesn't only effect decisions you make about horizontal positioning, it pertains to vertical as well. In this case researchers were interested in whether rational messages about facts and figures should appear highest on a page, or whether emotional messages should lead(62).

Their guess? Rational, head-based messages would be more easily processed when on the top of the page and emotional, heart-based messages lower down because this is consistent with how our bodies are designed - the head is higher than the heart.

And that's what they found.

> *"For example, in a granola bar advertisement, the words "a tasty choice" are best placed below a picture of the treat, because "tasty" makes an emotional appeal, whereas the words "the healthy choice" (a more rational culinary claim) are best placed above the picture. Another example: A sports car (generally a more emotional purchase) may promise to "fulfil your dreams" — words that should be placed lower in the commercial. By contrast, a more practical vehicle may advertise, "Save money by increasing gas mileage," a more rational claim that would be placed higher up to achieve the greatest effect in potential consumers."*

While the researchers were at pains to point to some caveats about this up/down, rational/emotion finding, such as the effect being reduced by brand, this research again shines a light on how the ease with which our customers process our messages has a large bearing on their effectiveness.

The key take away for us is that effective communications tend to mirror representations of our physical world. Any deviation to this interferes with our ability to process the information in a fluid and constructive way, and inhibits our engagement with the subject matter.

6. Get Now Me on board

Messages that promise instant gratification for Now Me are generally persuasive. A straightforward technique to use, messages like "Download this instantly!", "Get your copy now!" and "Instant access!" are ideal if yours is a product that can deliver immediate benefits. Even beauty products have a go, promising you'll "See visibly younger skin in just 7 days[63]", get "Instant skin smoother[64]" and that their product "Instantly reduces the look of fine lines, dark spots, uneven skin tone[65]".

But what if you are in the business of getting people to take action today for a benefit that will be experienced at a future time? Say anti-smoking, superannuation, education, fitness, nutrition, or financial planning?

You'll need to come up with ways of either gratifying or overcoming Short-Term Bias - getting Now Me on board.

Let's take two Australian Government Quitline ads as a study in contrasts for dealing with Now Me behaviour.

The first example, "A Little Bit of Suffering Saves a Whole Lot of Suffering Later" tells the smoker that they should endure a little bit of suffering in the short-term (i.e. headaches, increased appetite) to avoid bigger issues down the track (i.e. stroke, mouth cancer).

While this is an entirely honest and rational ad, the problem is Now Me doesn't like bad news, and will prefer to leave the risk of bad stuff happening to the distant Future Me. Now Me would rather avoid a headache when they have a big meeting tomorrow or avoid an increased appetite if they are dieting for a wedding than reduce their odds of cancer down the track.

By way of contrast, another Quitline ad called "Stop Smoking, Start Repairing" works to entice Now Me by promising benefits within a short period. In the ad a man (or woman) is staring directly at us while sitting on a medical gurney. Call out text boxes surround the image informing us what the reformed smoker can look forward to.

"In 12 months your risk of heart disease has halved", "In 12 weeks your lungs regain the ability to clean themselves" and, most importantly for Now Me, "In 1 week your sense of taste and smell improve". Suddenly Now Me can see a short-term benefit to quitting and will be more likely to take action.

Encouraging smokers to quit is not the only hot bed of Now Me behaviour. Financial institutions too have a struggle on their hands to get people to do things now for a benefit down the track.

Westpac New Zealand was grappling with how to get people to put more money into their savings rather than on-call bank accounts. Identifying Now Me's desire for immediate gratification, they created their "Impulse Saver App" to capitalise on the fleeting thought customers have that they should save more(66). As soon as the urge strikes Westpac customers can click the App, press a giant red button and a pre-defined amount of money is transferred from an on-call account to their savings account with higher interest.

The App has exceeded uptake expectations and generated hundreds and thousands of dollars in free media(67).

One Australian superannuation provider has also tried to bridge the Now Me-Future Me divide. Alongside the more distant benefits of superannuation, Care Super promote on their website that they are

"Helping you now", telling customers they can use their superannuation immediately for life and disability insurance cover(68).

A little more ambitiously, researchers have been testing ways of getting Now Me to take action on Future Me's behalf through use of empathy(69).

Noting that Now Me finds it difficult to imagine Future Me, researchers took an image of each participant and digitally aged it to look like they may when they need to rely on their superannuation. The results were promising. People were more likely to contribute more to their superannuation when they were looking at an older version of themselves.

7. What others do

We covered earlier how the physical environment can shape behaviour, but the social environment can too through Social Norms. Social Norms are a short cut to what we can trust; just think about landing in an unfamiliar place and trying to decide where to eat – do you go to the empty restaurant or the one with people in it?

As we've already identified, Social Norms can be a barrier to behaviour. The flip side is they can compel behaviour too. For instance, research into Social Norms has shown that:

* People were 30% more likely to buy food on a plane if their neighbour did(70)
* Energy consumption was cut by 2% when people received their bill comparing their use to that of their neighbours(71)
* £5.6 billion in overdue tax revenue was collected by the UK government when people received a letter telling them that 9/10 people paid theirs on time(72)

The lesson is therefore to *normalise the desired behaviour.*

Of course, drawing on the Social Norm is straightforward when the majority of people are already doing what you want. But what if yours is not popular or you are launching something new?

Let's take Facebook for example. Facebook wasn't always the Social Norm, so how does a site developed in a college dorm room become something used by over 1.59 billion active users per month(73)?

Founder Mark Zuckerburg and his team understood the power of **exclusivity**. Originally only available to students of Harvard, the site was then opened up to other universities, then high schools before becoming accessible to anyone with an email address(74).

In other words, one of the opportunities to use Social Norms to advantage is to segment and cascade availability. Create a buzz around a cohort of early adopters and deny access to other groups, at least in the early stages. Once the product or service's perceived popularity is robust, the walls can come down.

We're persuaded by others but don't like to think we are

A special warning about Social Norms. While we are influenced by what we see or understand others do, we don't respond well to being told to follow the herd because it interferes with our sense of uniqueness.

That means you should not point out to a customer that they are doing something because everyone else is.

---

8. Framing

Framing is the context you provide around your offer – how you "frame" it. In effect, how you describe something you sell.

Take one restaurant who changed the description of a menu item from "Broccoli" to "Seasoned Asian broccoli" and saw sales increase 27%(75).

Or perhaps you are up for some surgery. Option A has an 80% chance of survival, and option B a 20% chance of mortality. If you are like most, I'm sure you'd prefer Option A(76).

As these examples illustrate, we are persuaded by things other than facts. How something is communicated can impact what we do.

Framing with Numbers Psychology

Behaviour can be impacted by the way in which a number is communicated. This is referred to as **Numbers Psychology**.

Lesson 1. Decimals make the number seem bigger

Here are two ads from my local paper for servicing your car. Disregard the price, but what do you notice about the number?

The one on the left uses decimals ($139.00), the one on the right does not ($199). Surprisingly this will have an impact on how that price is perceived because decimals elongate the number.

Keen to understand how consumers perceive price points, researchers ran a series of experiments varying whether the price included a comma and/or decimals(77). They found that commas (e.g., $1,599 vs. $1599) or cents (e.g., $1599.85 vs. $1599) lead people to perceive the number to be bigger. Why? It seems we spell the number out in our heads and equate more syllables with numerical magnitude.

The take away is that when you want a number to look more impressive (e.g. salary increase, bonus or prize), use commas and decimals, but when you want to diminish the number (e.g. price or fee), don't.

Lesson 2. Numbers to the left stick in the mind

Why is $19.99 so much more compelling than $20? And is it?

One of the most popular elements of pricing to research is what's called the "Left-Digit Effect". That is, why the numbers to the left of the decimal are more influential than those to the right.

In one study the researchers concluded that "Shoppers pay a disproportionate amount of attention to the leftmost digits in prices and these leftmost digits impact whether a product's price is perceived to be relatively affordable or expensive[78]."

And in another, "We show that nine ending prices may sometimes but not always be perceived to be lower than a price one cent higher. This perception is more likely to occur when introducing a nine ending in the price causes a change in the left-most digit[79]." So $19.99 is perceived as lower than $20.00.

In fact a meta-analysis of 100 pricing studies lead one researcher to conclude it's not the last number on a price tag that makes a difference, it's the first. "People focus more on the left-most digit. Just-below pricing certainly makes it seem like the price is less than it actually is. It gives an image of being a bargain or a discount[80]."

But this same researcher also found "it can give the image that an item is of low or questionable quality", so should be used with caution.

One theory as to why this is the case relates to mental rehearsal, and that when we see a number we sound it out in our mind. Saying "fourteen" rather than "fifteen" makes us perceive the price is lower. As an example, if I were to ask you how much petrol is at the moment (say 134.99) I expect you will recite to me the numbers to the left of the decimal (i.e. 134) rather than round up to the full number (i.e. 135).

The lesson? There is such a thing as the left digit effect. But…

Lesson 3. Rounding your price can signal readiness to sell

Rounded prices have a role to play too. According to a recent study which analysed over 10.5 million eBay "Best Offer" listings, rounded number (e.g. $200) listings[81]:

* received offers approximately 6 to 11 days sooner on average than precise-number listings (e.g. $196) and

* were 3%-5% more likely to sell than precise-number listings.

However, these rounded number listings attracted lower offers and sold at prices that were 5%-8% **lower** on average than nearby precise-number listings.

According to the researchers, the rounded prices were a 'cheap-talk' signal, with much the same impact as '9' (e.g. $99, $8.99) has been used. Sellers who used precise-number listing prices went on to bargain more aggressively, while sellers who used round numbers were more likely to settle and made less aggressive counter-offers.

Further, use of precise numbers (like $12.37) can infer that a lot of thought has gone into the price point, whereas a rounded number seems less determined[82]. This even extends to salary negotiations, where researchers suggest you are better to use a precise number because it seems more assured.

So, rounded numbers can play a role in price signalling, particularly when used to stand out against other non-rounded price points, but precise numbers have their role to play too.

Lesson 4. Smaller font infers lower price

Walk into most shops and this is how they display their mark down:

Was $9.00
Now $5.99

Seems reasonable enough doesn't it, having the original price listed but then grabbing attention with the new lower price?

Turns out that this might not be the best way to communicate the deal.

Researchers wanted to understand whether the relative difference in font size between the old and new price had a bearing on how it was perceived(83).

It did.

As they discovered, signs that carried the lower price in smaller font relative to the original sold 28% more. It's better for the sign to have the marked down price in smaller font relative to the original as follows:

This is known as the **"size congruency effect"** and as the researchers noted, "presenting the lower sale prices in relatively small font resulted in more favorable value assessments and greater purchase likelihood or choice than presenting the lower sale prices in relatively large font."

And further, "the manner in which comparative price information is displayed can potentially be even more important than the magnitude of the price reduction itself (depending, of course, on price-elasticity of demand) in driving product sales."

> **Consider the distance of signage**
> A word of caution before you race off and change your signage to smaller/larger typeface.
>
> Consider the distance from which your sign needs to be read because if all your customers can read is the larger original price then you may not entice people to find out more.

Framing through sequence and positioning

We've just read how font size relativity can impact perception of value. Let's now dive into how relativity itself can be a factor through what's known as **Anchoring**.

Anchoring means that the first value seen has an undue influence on how subsequent values are perceived. In effect we become anchored to the first value as the primary reference point.

With this in mind, think about how best to sequence a wine list to encourage higher priced wine to sell.

Option 1 lists the wines on a basis other than price (e.g. region, varietal), option 2 from lowest to highest and option 3, highest to lowest.

1.		2.		3.	
Wine A	$35	Wine B	$18	Wine D	$62
Wine B	$18	Wine A	$35	Wine C	$45
Wine C	$45	Wine C	$45	Wine A	$35
Wine D	$62	Wine D	$62	Wine B	$18
No sequence		Lowest to highest		Highest to lowest	

Thanks to Anchoring, we know that option 3 will most successfully persuade people to purchase higher value wine because Wine D at $62 provides a high cost anchor. While they may not purchase D, suddenly C at $45 seems quite reasonable relative to $62.

Option 2, on the other hand, anchors people at $18 and things only get more painful as they work their way down the list. While they may not opt for the cheapest wine at $18, they may stretch to $35.

And the no-price sequence Option 1? Well, in this case you're leaving the choice up to the consumer so anything could happen!

While Anchoring sounds easy, and in practice is straightforward to implement on things like menus and price lists, it's trickier when the anchor has been set and you need to adjust it.

Toyota's Prius motor vehicle is a case in point. Originally aimed at buyers looking to save on running costs, the Prius suffered because it was more expensive than alternatives in the 'economical car' market (i.e. the existing price anchor). Therefore, to support the higher price positioning, Toyota shifted to environmentally conscious customers and included features that no-frills competitors did not offer(84). By doing so Toyota re-anchored

Prius as a more expensive car, changing the pricing context in which it was judged.

Other examples of businesses that worked hard to separate themselves from the prevailing anchor include:

   * Starbucks avoiding comparison with inexpensive diner coffee. To re-anchor their prices Starbucks positioned their stores as a place out of home to spend time with friends, listening to interesting music and smelling freshly ground beans.

   * Red Bull avoiding comparisons with Coke and Pepsi. A differently shaped and sized can, and functional (energy) rather than aspirational (sexiness) benefits were central to red Bull's re-anchoring success.

Apple had a different anchoring problem when it brought the iPad to market – how to help people understand that the product was good value when there was no frame of reference? Should we be comparing it to a laptop? A smartphone?

This is how they handled it(85). In the launch presentation then CEO Steve Jobs announced the price as $999. Was this good? Bad? How on earth do you know? You could almost hear the murmur as people tried to work out whether something they'd never seen or imagined before was worth $999.

But just as people were getting warmed up Jobs pulled a masterstroke.

The $999 emblazoned on a slide was dramatically 'smashed' by a new price taking its place. $499. It took Jobs mere moments to anchor people to $999 and then delight them with the "low" price of only $499.

Consider this. He could have started and ended with $499 in which case people would have been asking the same questions as they were at $999.

Is it good value? What do I compare it with? Jobs influenced perception of value by simply orchestrating the sequence of price information.

And it's not only the sequence of pricing that can make a difference. You'll recall from strategy 5. Mirror the Body that researchers have discovered something called "**Up/down congruence**(86)", where factual messages were better placed higher than emotional ones because it is consistent with our head being higher than our heart.

Researchers have also found that if you include before and after pictures it is better to have the before on the left because this is consistent with representations of past-left and future-right(87). It was found that:

   * people naturally relied on the past-left, future-right representation and used the horizontal position of the images in their evaluation of the products.

   * for self-improvement products like weight loss (and services like cosmetic procedures) participants had a more positive attitude toward the product when the advertisement displayed before images on the left and after images on the right.

   * when participants were primed to want a modern product for home decoration, they were more favourable when it appeared on the right side of the advertisement whereas when they were primed to desire an antique, they were more favourable when the product appeared on the left.

   * when there was no shopping goal (i.e. not primed for modern or antique), and therefore time was not relevant, the position of the image didn't impact judgment.

   * for people who read left to right, past-left and future-right was important whereas those who read right to left (e.g. Hebrew) the pattern was reversed.

Framing using symbols

While numbers are a special type of symbol, let's look at some other ways we can contextualise information to engage our customers.

Dollar signs

Let's imagine you are a café owner who is writing up the specials for the day on your trusty blackboard. You have a choice to make. Should you include the dollar sign or not?

According to researchers at Cornell University diners who ordered from a numeral-only menu spent significantly more than those who had menus that included dollar signs(88). The theory is that dollar signs trigger negative associations with the pain of paying, so the absence of such a symbol serves to diminish this aversion.

By the way, contrary to expectation, they did not find that word-based (e.g. fifteen) rather than numeral-based (15.00) menus resulted in higher sales.

The lesson here is to drop the dollar sign wherever possible. Where you do need to convey that the number is a price point, consider communicating it in a table or row header rather than right next to the number so that you reduce the psychological connection.

Smiley faces

Speeding motorists are a problem in most countries. Rather than rely on a traditional mix of speed cameras, public education and fines, a council in Scotland thought outside the box. Two hundred and twenty six electronic speed recording signs were installed that not only displayed the speed of the car, but included either a smiley or sad face according to whether the driver was under or over the limit. Under the speed limit? Smiley face. Over the limit? Sad face. It sounds ridiculous but it's claimed the initiative has reduced speeding by 53%*(89)*.

The secret behind the effectiveness of a smiley face is something with which you are familiar: Social Norms. A smiley face communicates whether the behaviour is socially acceptable.

It's not just speeding. Smiley faces have also been used to endorse the power-saving activity of residents in the US*(90)* - resulting in a 2% reduction in consumption - and to improve the perceived likeability of the sender of an email*(91)*.

Behavioural Economics in practice

Let's bring together what we've learnt so far about Framing to improve the effectiveness of this sign for a breakfast offer.

Assuming $15 for breakfast is an attractive deal (otherwise it would be strange to promote it) what could this business have done differently?

$14.90 rather than $15.00
Mental rehearsal means that "fifteen" sounds more than "fourteen". For the sake of a few cents this business could therefore go with a $14.90 or $14.95 big breakfast offer.

$15 rather than $15.00
However if this business was adamant it wanted to go with $15 then there's something else it can do. We know that decimals elongate the number, taking us longer to process and leading to a perception that the number is bigger than it actually is, so in this case we could simply go with $15 rather than $15.00 making the number seem shorter.

By the way, should they go with $14.90 or $15? The mental rehearsal of a lower number will still trump decimals so I'd go with a slightly lower price.

Use of dollar sign

As we've discovered, in menu design it is a good idea to drop the dollar sign. However in this case because the business needs to signal that 15 is the price as distinct from an item number, address or the quantity of breakfasts, the dollar sign is doing its job appropriately. That it is small relative to the number is also a good move because it deemphasies the price signal.

***

We started this chapter with a discussion of Apathy and how a failure to interest your customer will fail to budge them from the status quo. Our task is therefore to understand the System 1 and System 2 dynamics at play and use different strategies to engage.

Whether we do this through Framing, making something easy, designing the environment or appealing to Now Me, your role is to shape the context so your customer is compelled to take action.

The problem, of course, is knowing how much to do without overwhelming your customer in the process. So let's now turn to understanding why offering too much choice can paralyse your customer.

Chapter 4. Paralysis

Tell me if this experience rings true. It's Christmas time and you've driven to your local shopping center. After circling for what seems like hours, you see some shoppers walking to their car and stalk them like prey. Relief floods over you as you finally squeeze your car into the space and set off to do your shopping.

Now imagine you have arrived early at a convention centre and the car park is completely empty. Where should you park? On an upper level or below? To the left or the right? By the entrance door or by the exit? In shade or away from trees?

If you are like most of us, the empty car park scenario is a frustrating excursion into the world of dithering. You are presented so many choices about where to park that it takes you longer to make a decision. By contrast, when your options are limited, like at Christmas time, just getting a space is far more important than one that is optimal. Anywhere will do!

In this chapter we are going to be talking about why more choice isn't necessarily a good thing, and how to avoid paralysing your customer with too many options.

As a case in point, let's look at the field of retirement savings in the US.

Retirement savings are not compulsory in the US, so businesses and financial institutions have had to look for ways to encourage employees to voluntarily set aside a portion of their income. Retirement (401k) plans therefore have to be attractive, leading some employers to expand the range and type of plans made available to staff. The theory goes that if employees can find a savings plan that suits their specific needs they will be more likely to join.

So despite such an array of options being available, why weren't more employees in these organisations taking out plans? Here's what researchers found: across over 800,000 US employees, more choice resulted in less participation*(92)*.

For firms who offered only two funds, participation rates peaked at 75 per cent. When 59 funds were offered, participation rates dipped to a low of approximately 60 per cent. On average, for every additional 10 funds available, the predicted individual participation probability declined by about 2 percentage points*(93)*.

What's going on here?

Well, just like the empty car park where it takes you longer to decide, employees were suffering from choice overload.

Choice overload is when we are faced with too many undifferentiated options for which we have no clear preference. The paradox is that we desire the freedom to choose but can get overwhelmed by it.

That is our second key barrier to getting people to change behaviour – **Paralysis.** The number of options may paralyse them.

The **Paradox of Choice** is illustrated in the following research*(94)*. Setting up a jam sampling station in a supermarket, researchers were interested in how the number of jams on display changed purchase behaviour.

Starting with 24 jams, 6 out of 10 people sampled and 3% went on to purchase. Then the experiment was repeated, but this time only 6 jams were presented. Now only 4 out of 10 people sampled the jams but of those, 30% went on to purchase., representing a tenfold increase in conversion.

It feels counter-intuitive, doesn't it? Provide less to get more. That's the paradox at work because if you ask people they will always say they want more choice.

Importantly, the paradox of choice is a hotly debated topic in behavioural science precisely because it is so counter-intuitive. In fact a meta-analysis across a range of choice studies was unable to offer conclusive proof that more choices always lead to less choosing[95].

This to me is the point of the paradox. We know that people like choice, but we also know that too many options can inhibit our ability to make a decision. The answer, I believe, lies not in necessarily reducing the options you offer, but in better structuring them so as not to paralyse your customer. After all, people turn to online retailer Amazon because of their extensive range, but can only use Amazon because of the way choices are structured.

> **Strike a balance**
> Striking a balance between the right number of options to attract interest and right number to get action requires consideration of your competitive landscape.
>
> Too limited and customers will go elsewhere, too expansive and they may get bamboozled.
>
> How options are communicated, including at what point they are revealed, becomes central to your success.

Why people seek more choice

There are a couple of conditions that incite the desire for greater choice.

Future Me likes variety

One of the characteristics of Future Me is that we like to keep our options open. **"Diversification Bias",** which we already met in Chpater 3, means we tend to overestimate our need for variety.

Diversification Bias was evident when researchers asked participants to choose from a selection of chocolate bars[96]. In one experiment, a group of subjects were required to choose one chocolate each week for three weeks (known as the "sequential condition"). Another group of subjects were instead required to choose three bars of chocolate at the one time to consume over three weeks (the "simultaneous condition"). The finding? Those who chose for their future self in the simultaneous condition overestimated their desire for variety by as much as 20%.

In other words, if people chose close to the time of consumption, they required less variety. When they were choosing for consumption in the future, they thought they would want more variety than they actually did.

This means that if you ask your customer about what options they might like in the future they will tend to ask for more than they end up using – another trap of System 2 answering a question that System 1 is more likely to answer.

Decision Quicksand

If you've ever been frustrated that a customer has sought out more and more information, but ended up further away from making a decision then you might be interested in **"Decision Quicksand".**

It turns out that when we think a decision is going to be easy – like which toothbrush to buy – but then get unexpectedly confused by the decision, we react by seeking out more information. The amount of time and effort we invest is typically equated with the importance of a decision, so if we find ourselves spending time on a low-grade decision we tend to elevate its importance in our minds.

As the researchers say: "people sometimes fall into a recursive loop between deliberation time, difficulty, and perceived importance. Inferences from difficulty may not only impact immediate deliberation, but may kick off a quicksand cycle that leads people to spend more and more time on a decision that initially seemed rather unimportant. Decision quicksand sucks people in, but the worse it seems, the more we struggle(97)."

For your customers, therefore, it means helping them through low-grade decisions so they don't get unnecessarily stuck in the mire of information. If something that seems easy is taking them a long time to decide upon try resetting their minds. Take the decision temporarily away from them before they look at it again with a fresh and clear perspective. Remove rather than add information to the decision process.

How businesses overwhelm customers

In our endeavours to be attractive and helpful to customers, we can inadvertently fall into the trap of overwhelming them. Let's look at the two things we shouldn't do when offering our customers choice.

1. Too many options

Imagine you have a sore tooth so you search online for an emergency dentist. You click to the most likely looking website and see their phone number in the top right corner. Then, just below that number is another phone number. Is it the same? Different? And just below that second phone number are all their social media icons – Facebook, Twitter, Google + and YouTube.

Let's take it back a step. This business is an emergency provider of dental care so their customers are likely to be under some duress and wanting a quick decision. It stands to reason that these customers are not going to want to have to decipher phone numbers and visit a Google+ hangout.

This business has lost its way, and in its efforts to be helpful and provide multiple points of contact has ended up providing too many, cluttering its site and confusing its customers.

Lesson number one when it comes to choice is to not provide superfluous options that distract the customer from their objective.

2. Undifferentiated options

A couple of years ago I was shopping online for a copy of Mark Twain's "Life on the Mississippi". Five versions were presented on the book retailer's website, each with a different cover image, publishing date and price.

The problem for me was working out on what basis to make the selection. Aside from price and cover artwork, how could I know whether one was better than the other? On what basis were the books differentiated? An easy decision just got more difficult.

When it comes to communicating options to our customers we need to explain why they are different. In the case of Life on the Mississippi, I knew the author was the same so in the absence of any other rationale provided by the retailer, my choice became one of artwork (not a big factor) and price (the deciding factor).

And this is the caution for you. When options are undifferentiated you risk your customers opting for the cheapest. And that's what I did.

How to help customers choose

If customers are likely to be paralysed by choice when you present too many or undifferentiated options, then clearly the solution lies in constraining options and communicating how they are different. For this we can use **"Choice Architecture"** which describes the deliberate design of how and how many choices are presented.

Let's get a bit more specific with five behavioural tactics that can help you clarify the decision for your customer.

1. What others do

We've encountered Social Norms already as a way to overcome Apathy. When we see that other people think something is good then we are more likely to take notice.

Social Norms also have a role to play in clarifying choices, as this business has demonstrated.

BASIC
Free

SELECT
$19 AUD per month*
* Billed $228 AUD annually
See monthly plan

GOLD *Most Popular*
$25 AUD per month*
* Billed $300 AUD annually

PLATINUM
$65 AUD per month*
* Billed $780 AUD annually

Four options are presented, but only one has been deemed the "most popular". While our cynical System 2 might question whether the business is being truthful, our System 1 will likely be influenced by this type of signal because when in doubt, we follow the herd.

> **Best seller lists**
> Best seller lists can be helpful for customers, particularly in a retail environment. If I don't know any better, the safest thing is to follow the decisions of others.

2. Defaults

How did New York taxi drivers generate an extra $144 million in tips in a year(98)? Did they;
   a. Stop carrying change
   b. Start introducing themselves by their first name
   c. Change the default tipping level on the payment screen

The answer is c. The change that generated millions in extra tips was to the default tipping levels, from 15/20/25% to 20/25/30%.

Now bear in mind that customers could override any of the preselected options and key in their own value, but most simply clicked the button. Why? Our Default Bias.

Default Bias is our tendency to go with the predefined option – the status quo – and from what we already know, status quo is difficult to displace.

You can therefore use defaults to your advantage when helping customers make choices. Instead of leaving options unchecked, preselect your preferred choice because it will increase the odds of it becoming your customer's choice too.

> **Deciding on the default option**
> Which option you choose as the default will depend on your objective.
>
> You may want to default the highest margin option, cheapest or the most popular.
>
> Just make sure you do this thoughtfully rather than leaving it to chance.

3. Relativity

Working for a large corporation a few years ago, I was content that I was getting a fair day's pay for a fair day's work. My world slightly titled however, when I found out I was being paid substantially less than my (male) colleagues. Suddenly I was not so content.

We assess the value and fairness of something in relative rather than absolute terms. In this case, while in absolute terms I was being paid adequately, in relative terms I was not.

When it comes to clarifying choices we can use relativity to differentiate value, helping the customer know where one option sits compared with another.

You may have experienced this when buying a house. A smart real estate agent may take you to an expensive house that is a bit run down before showing you through a similarly priced house that doesn't require renovation. The second house seems a great choice relative to the first.

And this can be the role played by what are known as **pricing decoys**. $99 crayfish on a menu makes $36 steak look like good value (thanks to Anchoring, which we learned about in Chapter 4 on Apathy). In this case the lobster is a decoy because it is not expected to be ordered; its role is to provide a context against which other options may be judged.

For you, what is your value being judged against? Should you introduce a pricing decoy to better contextualise the value of your products and services?

4. Display

How you choose to display options will have a large bearing on which is selected. Based on a real example I saw online, take a look at the image below and tell me which option you think they want customers to select?

Design

It's pretty clear that they are nudging customers to the middle option, aren't they? Using design elements such as boxing and shading and by making bigger, this business is pulling focus to the centre. Knowing what we do of default bias this will make it more difficult for people to move away and consider the other options.

Not only that, this business has used Anchoring with the most expensive option as the first number to the left, and they've included a "Best Value" cue to further reinforce the preferred choice.

Centre Stage Effect

The other strategy employed by this business is to offer only three options. The advantage of using an odd number, and specifically three, is that people tend to choose the middle option. Known as the **"Goldilocks"** or **"Centre Stage Effect"**, researchers have found people prefer to avoid extremes, and instead cluster around the middle(99). This effect has been found to occur both in vertical (top to bottom) and horizontal (left to right) formats.

Does that mean you never use an even number of options? Two or four? No. An odd number is better when you want the customer to decide 'which' option to choose (which tie should I wear?), whereas an even number is better for 'this or that', binary choices (hot or cold, left or right, up or down, blue suit or black?).

Power of three

Not only do three options tend to influence people to choose from the middle, it has also been found that you should limit yourself to three points of substantiation when communicating your value[100].

Any more than that and people will think you doth protest too much!

Hierarchy of actions

Decisions about how to display options in an online environment should help customers understand which action is more important than another. To do this you need to establish a hierarchy of Call to Actions (CTA).

In the figure below you'll see that example A presents each Call to Action (button) as equally important. The customer is not cued to take one action over the other. However, let's say you want them to Buy Now. Example B differentiates the buttons and uses a brighter, more engaging colour for Buy Now to attract attention. It is also on the right of the other button, signalling progress. Option C also emphasises the Buy Now button, providing a secondary Call to Action through the More Information hyperlink.

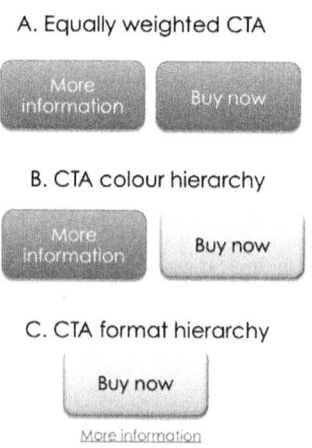

A. Equally weighted CTA

B. CTA colour hierarchy

C. CTA format hierarchy

You'll note that in all three examples we have provided the same number of choices for the customer (two), but we have cued them differently and will therefore influence behaviour in a different way.

5. Constrain choices

Constraining the number choices you offer is another way you can reduce choice overload. I review a lot of websites in the course of my work and was struck by the contrast in approach between two Content Marketing firms.

The first used a tiled design, with their home page covered by about 24 square images. As you hovered over each tile it flipped over to reveal what it represented. It felt like playing the card game 'fish' where you were partaking in some kind of mad lucky dip. It was impossible to know where to start or where to go next. It was frankly exhausting and I couldn't wait to exit the site. (They have subsequently ditched this design).

The second used a much cleaner design, with a clear value proposition in black typeface on a white background. Only two actions were suggested – to watch their video or click the Free Registration button. What a relief! Simplicity.

While it seems counter intuitive to give your customers fewer options, constraining choices can help them because it requires them to expend less energy trying to wrap their heads around what you are communicating.

It's not without risk, however, because you have to be clear on what to hold back and what to retain. In other words, you have to be clear on your value. What are your customers really looking for?

As we've discovered, choice is one of the trickiest areas to get right in business.

* Too many options or options that are undifferentiated will tend to paralyse your customer.

* Insufficient choice and you might not attract them in the first place.

It means rather than relying on a 'more is better' approach, which can be expensive in terms of inventory management and marketing, we have to be disciplined about how many options we present and how we present them.

Help your customer by refining the choice set, displaying options in a way that differentiates, tell them what other people choose and of course, provide a default for them to fall back on.

Balancing the need to attract with the need to decide

You'll remember from the jam study that when more jams were presented, more people sampled but fewer went on to purchase.

This suggests people are indeed attracted to a larger choice set, but when it comes to a decision, can get overwhelmed.

The art in business is to therefore promote sufficient choice to attract customers but then structure the choice process so it seems manageable.

Something we haven't yet talked about is what may be underpinning Paralysis; fear about making the wrong choice. So let's turn our attention to how we can overcome the final barrier to getting customers to take action.

Chapter 5. Anxiety

Why is tennis great Roger Federer's second serve average only 152 kms/hour when his first serve is 186 kms/hour*(101)*? The balls are the same. The court is the same. The opponent is the same. What's changed? What's at stake.

Tennis is an intriguing sport because players get a 'do over' on their serve. If their first serve doesn't go in the court of play it is called a fault and they get a second chance. Only when their second serve fails do they lose the point.

For this reason the second serve looks quite different to the first. Where the first is typically hard, fast and close to the line, the second tends to be more conservative; slower, softer and allowing a greater margin of error.

What you are witnessing in a game of tennis is the behavioural principle of **Loss Aversion**; we are more motivated to avoid a loss than seek a gain.

Loss Aversion

To my mind the most powerful principle in Behavioural Economics, Loss Aversion has rewritten the rules on how to influence behaviour.

While for years we've believed the hype that people love to win, in actual fact we love to avoid losing more. Losing means giving up something we already have, and the **Endowment Effect,** where we place a greater value on things we own, means we prefer to avoid this scenario.

Let me show you with the flip of a coin. If it lands on heads you'll win $100 but if it lands on tails, you'll lose $100. Interested? Probably not because you stand to lose as much as you stand to gain.

Loss Aversion tells us that in order for me to get you to take the bet, I would have to raise your gain by as much as 2.5 times the loss*(102)*.

In other words, for me to get you to give up your known position – the status quo – for the chance of whatever gain I am offering, you need that gain to be around double the loss. So if you risk losing $100 on tails but could gain $250 on heads you might be much more interested.

> **Double or nothing**
> The potential upside of the gain has to be double the risk of the loss.

Loss Aversion can make or break your business. It's the number one killer of conversion. If your customer is too scared to take action – too scared to leave the comfort of the status quo - they simply won't. Your task is therefore to identify what's making your customers anxious so you can mitigate its effects.

Three types of Anxiety: PES-imistic

When it comes to understanding what is making customers nervous we can look in three domains, Psychological, Economic and Social.

P - Psychological Anxiety

Each of us navigates the world according to a set of values and behaviours. When things conflict with this internal narrative we can get anxious due to **Cognitive Dissonance** and will take steps to either change the story or avoid the situation that brings us into conflict. Ask yourself how does what you are asking fit with your customer's view of the world? Does it conflict with their values?

E - Economic Anxiety

The most obvious form of Anxiety is related to cost – what does your customer stand to lose financially? What other resources do they have to commit, including time and effort? What is their opportunity cost that may persuade them not to go forward with you?

S - Social Anxiety

We are social creatures, and any decisions we make can be judged by others. What risk to your customer's social credibility does this pose? Will they lose face if this goes badly? To whom do they have to justify the decision – their boss, husband, wife, investors, staff?

Read between the lines
A customer will rarely tell you they are too scared to proceed.

Instead they'll cite objections like price or timing, so it's up to you to anticipate that Anxiety will be there, somewhere below the surface, and devise ways of negating it.

How businesses cause customer Anxiety

In our excitement about what the benefits to our customers will be, Anxiety can be easy to overlook. Our enthusiasm may cause us to inadvertently trigger fear in our customers and reduce the likelihood of them taking the deired action. Here are four things we shouldn't do.

1. Too much

Have you ever purchased a pair of shoes online and been asked for your date of birth? I have. That it was part of the account set up is beside the point – there is no reason for this business to ask such an invasive question and it put me on the back foot.

When we get greedy and ask for **too much** from our customers we risk losing them. While it might be useful to know the age profile of your customers, Date of Birth is a particularly sensitive piece of information. A softer approach would be to ask for day and month only (if the purpose is to reward for their birthday), or month and year only (for demographics).

Another mistake is to ask for an email address without telling your customer why. If you don't clarify why it's required your customer will get anxious about being spammed. It would be better to tell them you need their email address to send them a confirmation of their order so they know why and what they get.

Strangely enough you can also trigger customer Anxiety by over playing your credentials. Researchers have found that including more than three points affirming your greatness can undermine the effectiveness of your proposition because it triggers scepticism(103). It's a case of 'doth protest too much'.

2. Too soon

Let's say you are in the market for a new bicycle and visit the store to start shopping around. One catches your eye so you want to take a closer look. Before you can even read about some of the features the shopkeeper is in your face asking whether you are ready to buy.

"Ahh, no I just got here. I haven't even had a chance to…"

It sounds ridiculous, doesn't it? If we encountered this kind of aggressive behaviour in a shop we would simply leave.

Why then do some retailers think it's okay online?

The image above is from the home page of an online bike retailer. You'll note that the (only) Call to Action is "Buy Now" which is inappropriate for this stage of the purchase process.

The retailer has escalated the commitment required by their customers **too soon**, and increased Anxiety as a result. We need to ask our customers to take action at a pace that suits the interaction, and not rush to the end-point before they are ready.

Know when to use 'Buy Now'

'Buy Now' is rarely an appropriate first Call to Action (CTA).

Exceptions might include products that are experienced offline and then purchased online (e.g. perfume) but it will be more prudent to use a "More information" or "Product details" CTA instead.

---

3. Too little

When a customer is appraising you, your shop or your website you have only seconds to form a good first impression*(104)*. What do I mean by a good impression? That they can trust you enough to hang around to find out more.

Remember that System 1 works at lightning speed, forming what we might call a 'gut reaction' before System 2 has even cranked into gear. While rationally you might have all the facts and figures to support their decision to do business with you, if your customer doesn't intuitively trust you it's going to be difficult to change their mind.

For this reason **too little** information about your credentials can poison your customer. Here's an example from a broadband provider.

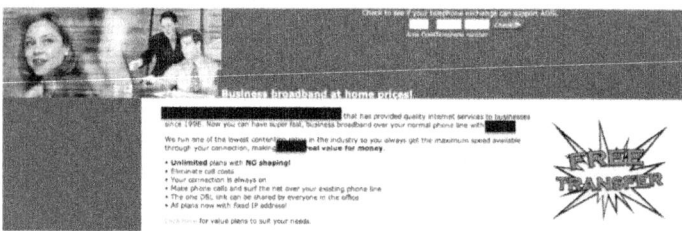

The failure to include a logo and the use of a cheap looking "free transfer" clipart graphic is likely to trigger alarm in potential customers. While they may not be able to put their finger on why, they will get the sense that this is a business to avoid.

Too little can also mean the absence of security icons and logos at the point of heightened Anxiety – the time of payment. The payment page for the business in the image on the next page could have been improved by simply adding such cues.

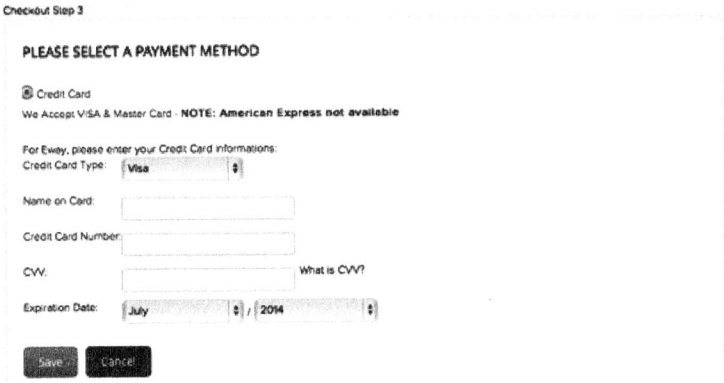

Checkout Step 3

PLEASE SELECT A PAYMENT METHOD

Credit Card
We Accept VISA & Master Card - **NOTE: American Express not available**

For Eway, please enter your Credit Card informations:
Credit Card Type: Visa

Name on Card:

Credit Card Number:

CVV: What is CVV?

Expiration Date: July / 2014

Save   Cancel

4. Too late

Some businesses have all the right things to say to reduce Anxiety but they leave them **too late.** They bury their accreditations and testimonials in literature or parts of their website their customer won't get to because they haven't been convinced upfront.

The art is to showcase your trustworthiness early without seeming arrogant and self-involved.

> **Humble brag**
> While it's important to include awards, affiliations, accreditations and testimonials to communicate your trustworthiness, balance this self-congratulation with statements about the problems you solve from the customer's point of view.
>
> Ideally, have others brag on your behalf.

Too much, too soon, too little, too late. These are four ways businesses escalate customer Anxiety and kill their chances of conversion. So what do you do to mitigate Anxiety? We're about to find out.

How to mitigate customer Anxiety

Now that we've identified how you might be making customers too anxious to proceed, let's talk about what to do about it.

There are two key strategies we can use. We can give customers:
1. nothing to fear
2. something to fear

1. Nothing to fear

Shine Hand Car Wash Cafe, a car washing business in Melbourne was struggling to convince customers to have their vehicles cleaned for fear it would rain soon thereafter. In other words, customers were too anxious to commit.

The answer? While they couldn't do anything about the weather, Shine Car Wash Cafe introduced a 24 hour rain guarantee that meant they would re-wash your car for free if it rained within 24 hours of your clean. According to the owner, Dalip Singh, "It is to encourage people to wash your car, even if it looks like raining. People are very happy as it takes out the guess work(105)."

In other words, they gave their customers **nothing to fear.**

Korean-made cars were new to the Australian market and consumers were wary. More specifically, customers were anxious about buying a new car without knowing what the re-sale value would be a few years down the track. Their "Now Me" was anxious about their "Future Me" getting ripped off.

The answer? Hyundai introduced their "Guaranteed Future Value" program that guarantees the future value of a new car*(106)*. Buy today knowing what you can get for the car when you trade-in in three years.

And that's not the only way Hyundai is giving customers nothing to fear.

It was 2009 and times were tough in the USA. The recession was hitting car manufacturers particularly hard but Hyundai was able to buck the trend and record growth in sales. How? They created the Hyundai Assurance program, a promise that they would buy back the car if their customer lost their job, went bankrupt or became disabled*(107)*. Over the 26 months the program ran, 1,000,000 cars were sold in North America with only 350 buy-backs. Here again Hyundai came up with a way to get customers to commit by giving them nothing to fear.

Which brings us to one of the most striking examples of how a business can mitigate fear resulting from Loss Aversion; the travel booking site Booking.com.

If you've ever booked accommodation online you'll know that it can be a heady mix of excitement and trepidation. The websites have to work pretty hard, therefore, to get us to commit rather than continuing to hunt for an even better deal.

Booking.com uses four elements on its 'room type' page to overcome the customer's fear of committing to the booking.
  * It starts by telling you there are no booking or credit card fees, reducing Anxiety about hidden additional costs
  * Then, rooms offering free cancellations are noted, reducing Anxiety about travel plans changing
  * The price is then presented marked down from it was originally (using Anchoring), reducing Anxiety about whether it is a good deal
  * And next to the Book now button are messages about only taking 2 minutes, or the fact that no registration is required, reducing Anxiety about the effort required in the booking process

The Melbourne car wash, Hyundai and Booking.com have shown us how taking fear off the table means your customers will be more likely to take the action you desire.

Of course these types of techniques should not be unfamiliar. Offering your product for free, free shipping, a generous returns policy and price match/beat guarantee are common strategies in market. Now you can not only identify them but also understand their role in thwarting Loss Aversion.

But there's more so let's now delve into "nothing to fear" strategies and tease out the specific behavioural principles we can draw upon.

Certainty

Imagine there are two strains of influenza doing the rounds so you decide to look into getting a vaccine.
   * Vaccine A will give you 100% protection against one strain of the flu but none against the other.
   * Vaccine B will give you 50% protection against each.

Which do you go for?

Most people prefer Vaccine A(108). Why? Because they can be certain that they are protected against at least one of the viruses and don't have to worry about that any more. Hedging bets with Vaccine B means they still have to worry about both.

Certainty plays a big role in behaviour because when we are unsure, we get anxious. When we get anxious, we tend to revert to the status quo.

Interestingly, the preference for certainty is related to whether the outcome is favourable or unfavourable.
   * If the outcome is expected to be positive, we prefer certainty (like avoiding the flu). We don't want to risk not receiving the good stuff.
   * In contrast, if the outcome is expected to be negative we prefer

uncertainty. We're happy to chance the odds if there's a slim possibility it will turn out okay.

With that in mind, here's a question I ask of workshop attendees*(109)*:

> An employer is under extreme financial hardship and may have to retrench as many as 600 staff.
>
> However there are still two options they can try.
>
> - If Option A is adopted, 400 jobs will be lost.
> - If Option B is adopted, there is a 33% chance that no jobs will be lost and a 67% chance that all jobs will be lost.
>
> Which option do you choose?

In groups I've run Option A, the certainty of a favourable outcome (200 jobs saved), was selected by 75% of participants with only 25% choosing Option B. That's a significant difference.

But here's the trick. Not all attendees received the same question. In fact, half the group received this variant of the same scenario:

> An employer is under extreme financial hardship and may have to retrench as many as 600 staff.
>
> However there are still two options they can try.
>
> - If Option A is adopted, 200 jobs will be saved.
> - If Option B is adopted, there is a 33% chance that all 600 jobs will be saved and a 67% chance that no jobs will be saved.
>
> Which option do you choose?

In this case, where Option A provided a certain unfavourable outcome (400 jobs lost), only 40% chose it with the 60% majority opting to chance a less certain outcome with Option B.

What's the difference?

While both scenarios presented the same results they were framed slightly differently. In the first version, the question was framed positively (jobs will be saved) and the second, negatively (jobs will be lost).

There are two key lessons from this exercise.

1. While certainty is a useful strategy to reduce Anxiety, it depends on whether the likely outcome is positive or negative, and

2. How you 'frame' a message can have a major bearing on the outcome you derive

Social Norms

Social Norms has cropped up in both Apathy and Paralysis, and here it is again in Anxiety. Social Norms gives us information about what the 'normal' behaviour is in a particular context. A fast way to reduce customer Anxiety about working with you is to therefore show them that other people trust you. In a practical sense, that means including testimonials and affiliations on your website and in your collateral.

> **Social media counters**
> Use social media counters with caution.
>
> If your following or shares are low this will become a form of negative social proof. I.e. you are signalling how unpopular you are!

Acceptance

You'll recall from the "PES-imistic" model of Anxiety that the "S" relates to the social context. In short, your customer will be asking himself or herself "how will I look to my boss/friends/spouse if this goes wrong?"

A feeling that we are accepted by those we value is a deep drive in all of us. As a business that means you can tap into the promise of **acceptance** to get your customer to take action.

Take car manufacturer Jeep's Australian TV ads*(110)*, for instance. The campaign featured a female buyer proudly announcing to her husband that she'd "bought a Jeep", reflecting our innate desire for social acceptance.

The key for you is to reduce your customer's Anxiety by helping them feel that those they regard will accept their decision.

Minimise upfront commitment

"Now Me" likes to have good stuff upfront and defer pain to "Future Me". Where possible, that means you should seek to minimise the magnitude of commitment required from your customer's Now Me so you get them on board.

A powerful example of this has been the "Save More Tomorrow" approach to retirement saving in the USA*(111)*. Realising that people saw putting money aside for retirement as an unpleasant sacrifice (hurting Now Me for the benefit of stranger called Future Me), behavioural economists Richard Thaler and Shlomo Benartzi devised a plan where people could agree to join today but not have any of their salary diverted until their next pay increase. By minimising upfront commitment the program helped increase the average rate of savings from 3.5% to 13.6% in just 3.5 years.

Minimise pain of paying

Nothing makes people more nervous than money. It is a very tangible expression of commitment, and means you need to reduce nervousness at the point of most obvious pain.

Aside from providing assurances like:
* a returns policy,
* professional looking invoice,
* security seals (like a padlock icon), and
* reputable credit card icons,

consider how the mode of payment can impact your customer.

The upshot is cash hurts more than credit because it is more vivid. In fact, according to researchers who were looking into the **pain of paying**(*112*):

* "The vividness of the money outflow leads to a higher pain of paying with cash than with other less transparent payment modes. In other words, the pain of paying is somewhat dulled by less transparent payment modes such as a gift certificate or credit card thus increasing the likelihood of spending when using these payment modes."

* "Consistent with previous research, this study demonstrated that people are willing to spend (or pay) more when they use a credit card than when using cash and the underlying reason for the differences in spending is, at least, partly due to differences in the pain of paying."

In short "less transparent payment forms tend to be treated like monopoly money and are hence more easily spent (or parted with)."

In speaking to the reasons credit cards dull the pain of paying, the researchers went on to say:

> *"there are two additional reasons that the pain of paying is dulled. First, the payment is temporally separated from the consumption. Second, credit cards allow mixing of purchases where several purchases are combined into one payment such that a single payment is not attributable to a specific consumption."*

Cash in your chips
Casinos use chips rather than cash for a reason – it disconnects the activity of gambling from the consequences of spending money.

Returns policy and guarantees

They've been mentioned before, but another way to give your customer nothing to fear is to offer them a generous **returns policy** or **money back**

guarantee. These policies work by eliminating the risk to the customer of the transaction not meeting their requirements.

But how generous do you need to be? Does the increase in sales outweigh the cost of increased returns?

To answer that question researchers undertook a meta-analysis of 21 related studies across over 11,600 subjects[113]. They found that while overall the more generous the returns policy the more likely it would be to increase returns, it would also be more likely to increase sales to a greater extent. So returns go up, but sales go up more.

2. Something to fear

The staff at café La Petite Syrah in Nice, France was tiring of rude customers[114]. Starting as a joke but has since become serious business, the café decided to introduce three different prices for coffee. When asking for coffee, customers who request "one coffee" with no please or thank you are charged 7 euro. A "please" or "thank you" drops the price to 4 euro 25, and "a Hello, one coffee please", a mere 1 euro 40. While the owner says he doesn't enforce the prices, it has improved the atmosphere in the café.

I've anglicised the menu in below.

Café prices

"A coffee" $7.00

"A coffee, please" $5.00

"Hello, a coffee please" $3.50

The café is shaping the behaviour of its customers by telling them they'll be worse off if they don't behave in a pleasant manner. They are giving them **something to fear.**

The flip side of giving people nothing to fear, and our second key strategy to mitigate Anxiety is to give our customers a reason to fear *not* taking action. In effect, the cost of inaction is greater than the cost of proceeding.

Let's say for example, you want to get lazy shoppers who have used your supermarket trolley to return it to the trolley bay. A tricky proposition because once you've carted your groceries to the car, the effort of returning the trolley exceeds any reward for doing so.

It turns out a dollar can make a difference. Most supermarkets now include a coin-release lock device on trolleys that means customers forfeit a gold $1 or $2 coin if they fail to return it. The supermarkets are using Loss Aversion to influence customers by giving them something to fear. It's not the amount of the money that's driving adherence, it's that the money belongs to the customer (**the Endowment Effect**).

Social Norms

Social Norms cropped up as a way to give your customers nothing to fear, and here it is again as a way of giving them something to fear.

Fear of Missing Out (FOMO) is one of the most compelling behavioural forces. The feeling of being left out or left behind is unpleasant, and can motivate people to take action. You can see it on display at retail sales events and overburdened train stations (and we'll discuss the role of scarcity in a minute).

Rejection

There's a sign in my gym for a deodorant that asks "Do you sweat more than normal?" Gee, I don't know…do I?

The ad is clever because it feeds on our fear of rejection; of being abnormal. We discovered how powerful acceptance can be in giving people nothing to fear – the counter point is the threat of rejection which can scare people into taking the desired behaviour.

Scarcity

A few pages ago we checked out how Booking.com was using four cues to reduce Anxiety and get customers to commit to the purchase. Well, here they are again, this time using Anxiety to encourage action. Booking.com and many other accommodation sites use words like "Last chance!" or "Last room" to create a sense of scarcity and get the heart pumping. Within the space of a computer screen the customer not only feels they have nothing to fear by making the booking, but now they have something to fear if they do not.

Scarcity is a fear inducing condition from our days as hunter-gatherers. When things are scarce, they become valuable. It works for diamonds, jobs, partners and real estate. And in Australia recently, baby formula. One business I saw used scarcity beautifully by using a pop-up online ad that read "Get 30% off. You'll never see this deal again". It's a clever way of capturing the customer's attention.

FIND A STORE

*Select styles only. While supplies last.
Limit 5 per customer

You can also cap the number of tickets or items you are selling in order to create a sense of scarcity, as the business on the previous page has done by placing a limit of five items per customer.

> **Positive and negative tension**
> To compel customers to take action you need to create positive tension and overcome negative tension.
>
> Positive tension is *the fear about missing out* on what's great about your offer, and you need this in order to create an appetite for change.
>
> Negative tension is *the fear about proceeding*, and this is what you need to mitigate in order to encourage action.

Framing and design

Two newspapers, two articles on the Australian Government's decision to appropriate unclaimed moneys sitting in inactive bank accounts. One carried the deadline "Dig up that buried treasure*(115)*", and the other, "Cash Grab: Inactive bank accounts to be seized*(116)*". Which is most likely to influence behaviour? The Cash Grab.

Framed as something to lose if you don't take action (use it or lose it), this headline taps into Loss Aversion. The buried treasure headline, on the other hand, speaks to an opportunity for a gain which, you now know, is far less motivating.

Similarly, UK phone provider's campaign poster carried the headline "You could be wasting £194 on the wrong phone tariff". Wasting? Ouch! They could just have easily have written "You could save £194..." but it simply does not have the same emotional impact.

How you frame your message is clearly very important.

> **A negative message doesn't have to be negative**
> You might be worried that using Loss Aversion and
> focussing on what people have to lose will make you
> sound too negative.
>
> One financial services client, for instance, was
> concerned the negativity would interfere with them
> being seen as friendly and approachable.
>
> The answer lies in framing the Loss Aversion message
> as being helpful. "We were worried you would miss out
> on..." for example.

Framing extends to how you design your communication. Here's a great real-life example of what you should do.

	FREE software	PRO software $29.95
Feature 1	✔	✔
Feature 2	✗	✔
Feature 3	✗	✔
Feature 4	✗	✔
Feature 5	✗	✔

Update   Upgrade

What do you notice about the offer?
   * The Free option is available, but has only one feature
   * The upgrade option has all five features
   * The "update" button for the free version is greyed out, making it seem like it doesn't work
   * The "upgrade" button is on the right (signalling progress) and presented in a stronger colour
   * Ticks and crosses are used to communicate at a glance the differences between the options.

The ad is designed to encourage customers to upgrade from the fee to paid software by spelling out the downside of the status quo. The customer can choose either, but this business has done a good job at giving them something to fear about sticking with the free version.

***

Of the three behavioural barriers, Anxiety is the one you have most control over. You've overcome Apathy and engaged your customer's attention – they want to do business with you. They are ready to make a decision, so Paralysis is not an issue. All that's left to do is dispel any fear they have about committing to you.

With the three barriers now conquered, and your newfound mastery of the Williams Behaviour Change Model to get your customers to take action, it's time to broaden our knowledge of how we can apply Behavioural Economics to common business issues.

In Part II of this book I have drawn on a selection of my most popular articles which deal with topics like market research, pricing, acquisition, retention, website design, people management and innovation.

If you've been wrestling with issues such as loyalty programs, cold calling, convincing internal stakeholders, motivating staff, and even whether Behavioural Economics can be used in Business-to-Business (B2B) and Business-to-Consumer (B2C) organisations, then you'll find answers in the following pages.

Part II.

Applied
Behavioural Economics

Chapter 6. Behavioral Economics by Business Type

Now that you've become familiar with the Williams Behaviour Change Model and the role of Behavioural Economics it's worth looking at whether it really is as flexible as we imagine. For instance, does it apply equally well in Business-to-Business (B2B) and Business-to-Consumer (B2C) contexts? Or for micro as well as macro challenges?

B2B vs. B2C approaches to behaviour

The most obvious application of Behavioural Economics is in consumer markets. As consumers ourselves, we are used to being 'influenced' by marketers.

But equally, in a B2B environment our job is to influence behaviour. While it may be a procurement manager rather than a shopper, we're still dealing with a human and all their foibles and non-rationalities.

So the short story is, yes, Behavioural Economics is as applicable in B2B as B2C environments because "people are people".

However, B2B typically has a more involved purchase cycle because your customer will need to get approval from others. That means there is a greater likelihood of them using System 2 to consider the decision. Less emotion, more facts. Remember, your customer is going to have to be your advocate, explaining to others the details of your offer so consider whether you have made this easy for them to do.

Added to that, B2B customers may feel further removed because it's not their money on the line, which can reduce the emotion.

For those in either a B2C environment or a role with direct connection with the customer (i.e. sales and marketing), focus is on the *end consumer*. The target is easily identified and everyone in the business tends to have a shared understanding of who you are trying to influence.

In a B2B environment or non-customer facing role it's a little different. We might be selling a product or service to an accountant, a teacher or a nutritionist, or 'selling' an idea to an investor, stakeholder, colleague or supplier. As a result we tend to think of them first by their profession rather than what they consume.

Here's how I summarise the differences in addressing the barriers to behaviour across B2B and B2C environments.

APATHY

B2C	B2B
• If your customer can't be bothered it will be hard to stimulate action. • They are likely to be buying for themselves or a loved one so will need to benefit directly from your offer	• Customers have been given the responsibility to take action. They may have to do this rather than want to. That doesn't necessarily make them engaged – they may be ticking boxes. • Reducing Effort is imperative because they are unlikely to persevere with a task they are not fully engaged with, particularly if a competitor is easier to deal with. • Reward may not be direct – they may not get to use product/service so they need to feel some sense of reward, even if that is recognition from you of their deft decision making. • Be careful about perception of favouritism or 'buying' their business through personal reward

PARALYSIS

B2C	B2B
• The customer will be making decisions based on their personal preferences.	• The customer has to consider other people's opinions and canvas sufficient options to demonstrate due diligence • Tabling the proposed solution alone will not work. Consider decoys and/or including options that have been discussed but discarded to demonstrate decision making process

ANXIETY

B2C	B2B
Your customer may be asking themselves: • "Is there a risk I'll lose my home or relationship over this?" • "How will I pay for this?" • "How will I look to my friends and family?"	Your customer may be asking themselves: • "Is there a risk I'll lose my job if this goes wrong?" • "How can I justify budget for this?" • "How will I look to my boss and colleagues?"

B2B vs. B2C learning approach to Behavioural Economics

The approach to learning about Behavioural Economics needs to be a little different across B2B and B2C businesses.

Same behavioural principles, different framework for application

While the behavioural principles are the same, in a B2C environment you need to focus on how your audience segment (your consumers) *receive* your message. In a B2B job function, on the other hand, your focus is on how to *send* your message.

B2C - how they receive your message
For those in B2C or customer facing roles, focus on how to apply Behavioural Economics to "them", the receiver of the message because it is natural to attend to their needs. From there the task is to retro-fit this understanding to how you craft your message.

In other words, because there is general consensus on who "they" are, you can use the Behavioural Change Model to work through solutions to the three behavioural barriers (Apathy, Paralysis and Anxiety).

B2B - how you send your message
In B2B or non-customer facing roles, you are dealing with individuals rather than a segment, so instead focus on how Behavioural Economics applies to you, the sender of the message. While your receiver might change *you* are the common element across all your attempts to influence.

The upshot of B2B is that while people are people and behaviour is behaviour, Behavioural Economics application is easiest when it feels familiar. That means adapting how it's done rather than what it does. Rather than relying on the Behaviour Change Model, you may prefer to use a How, Who, Where and When framework to incorporate behavioural principles.

What we're talking about is augmenting your rationally focused "what" and "why" of the project with the How, Who, Where and When from a non-rational perspect'

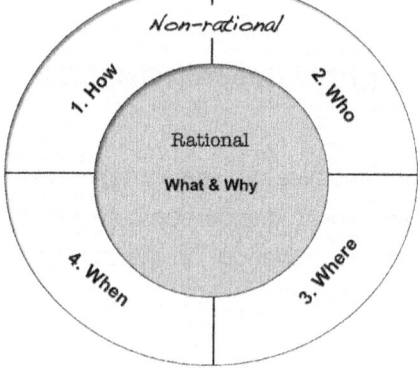

1. How

How you communicate matters. For instance, you get to choose whether you describe an opportunity as one to "save $10,000" or to "stop wasting $10,000". While both have the same value from a rational perspective, the second uses Loss Aversion which has much greater emotional impact.

Behavioural Principles to apply to **How**:

   * Relativity – What is the frame of reference for this decision? With what are you being compared?

   * Framing – How have your contextualised the options? Is it framed as a win or the avoidance of a loss?

   * Anchoring – To what value is your decision-maker anchored? Do you need to re-anchor them?

   * Loss Aversion – What does your decision-maker stand to lose if they proceed? If they don't?

2. Who

What others are doing matters. Your decision-maker will be persuaded by who you are and what other decision-makers might do.

Behavioural Principles to apply to **Who**:
    * Social Norms – Have you normalised the desired behaviour?
    * Authority – Have you presented yourself as the authority in this field?
    * Uniqueness – Have you preserved the decision-maker's sense of uniqueness?

3. Where

The environment in which the decision is made matters too. High or low ceilings, circular or angular seating, choice of typeface, noise levels and lighting can all impact decisions without the decision-maker being consciously aware.

Behavioural Principles to apply to **Where**:
    * Priming – Have you selected a location that supports your objective?
    * Choice Architecture – Have you made the preferred option the easiest to access?

4. When

The time horizon matters. People are driven by short-term needs and will be more persuaded by short-term benefits and deferred costs. They will also make different decisions depending on the time of day you approach them.

Behavioural Principles to apply to **When**:
    * Short-term Bias – Have you given them a benefit in the immediate term?
    * Ego Depletion – It's harder to break away from status quo when fatigued. If you want change, is your decision-maker fresh?

Based on article originally published: 23 February 2015
http://www.briwilliams.com.au/articles/Blog--News-Is-Behavioural-Economics-applicable-to-B2B-as-well

Chapter 7. Market Research and Customer Insights

How can it go so wrong when research says it's right?

Two companies. Two well intended product changes. Two expensive and embarrassing examples of how failing to understand real-world behaviour can backfire.

I'm Glad I'm not Milo

GLAD wrap and Milo were in the news in 2015 for the wrong reasons. GLAD introduced a new method of cutting their cling wrap, moving the cutter from an exposed blade on the box to one that was mounted on the lid.

Nestle changed the recipe of their malted chocolate drink Milo in New Zealand, removing vanilla and changing the mix of vitamins.

In both cases, people got very upset and called for boycotts. The companies were left scrambling to placate their consumers and shore up their market share.

As a past product manager I felt their pain. Making changes to a product is no easy thing, and would have followed extensive business justification and research.

In fact when interviewed a spokesperson for GLAD had this to say(117):

> "Before making these changes, GLAD completed rigorous and extensive in-home research in Australia. The results were

overwhelmingly positive favouring the changes including the movement of the cutter bar to the lid, with the safety aspect of this front of mind. In fact, more than 60% of those Australians, who participated in the research, preferred the improved product overall."

So why is there such a chasm between what businesses think their consumers want and what they actually do?

It seems businesses are doing one of three things:
1. getting the wrong kind of research,
2. ignoring what the research is really telling them or
3. cherry picking research to support a decision they want to make

1. Getting the wrong kind of research

If you are relying on what consumers tell you they want, don't.

It doesn't work for predicting the outcome of elections and it doesn't work for product development. Examples of this 'say vs. do' gap include;
   * 60% of US voters claiming they'll turn out to vote but only 40% do[118]
   * 50% of Victorians saying they eat healthily but only 7% eat their vegies[119]
   * Americans claiming they love Guinness but actually buy Bud Light[120]

It doesn't work because asking people in focus groups, surveys or interviews to tell you why they did or would do something engages their System 2 rationalising, slow thinking, cold state brain. It means you'll get a well intentioned justification of past behaviour or well intentioned rationalisation of future behaviour.

Such answers might look great in a research report and can be used as handy stats to quote in Press Releases, the problem is System 2 is unlikely to be the one making the decision to use or buy your product. System 1, our fast-thinking, impulsive, short-cutting, habitual, hot-state brain is the one who makes most of the decisions everyday.

Unfortunately it's not easy to ask System 1 what is likely to happen in the future. Merely asking the question prompts System 2 to take over.

Behavioural Economics helps you resolve this difficulty in two ways by providing:
    * a system of creating experiments in observable rather than self-reported behaviour so you don't have to ask, you can watch and
    * a framework of predictable factors that influence behaviour so you can anticipate what people are likely to do in a given set of circumstances

2. Ignoring what the research is telling them

When you are a product manager your role is to make the product better, and as the expert you spend a lot of time and energy thinking about it. In fact, more time than your consumer ever would.

And that's a problem because you develop ideas about what changes you should make, commission research about those changes and, thanks to **Confirmation Bias**, look for results that support rather than disaffirm your views.

Compounding this, the effort you have expended heightens your sense of ownership, making walking away mighty hard due to **Sunk Cost** - your desire to hold out for a return on the investment you've made.

How do you stop yourself from ignoring what research is telling you? Structure the research to disaffirm your hypothesis, looking for reasons not to do what you want to do, and make sure the decision not to proceed with a change is as valid as proceeding so you won't feel the pain of wasted effort.

3. Cherry picking research

Where ignoring research can in part happen subconsciously thanks to Confirmation Bias, cherry picking is more deliberate. This is about trawling the results to find anything that justifies a decision already taken, and sadly for consumers, researchers and business culture, all too common. I've done it in the past and I'm not proud.

How to prevent cherry picking? Too big a topic to tackle here because it gets to the politics of an organisation and its culture - the Social Norms at play and people's fear of failure. At the very least you can interrogate the research and ask to see the full story, reminding yourself that in today's world of social media the claims you go to market with are subject to relentless scrutiny.

Who you need to understand best

To avoid the situation Milo and GLAD have found themselves in, you need to know two people best.
   * Know thy consumer
   * Know thyself

To "know thy consumer" make sure your research includes a behavioural analysis, drawing on observed as well as (or instead of) self-reported behaviour.

And to "know thyself", create safe guards to compensate for you and your team's humanness - your biases and decision-making heuristics - because otherwise you risk setting yourself up for failure.

Based on an article originally published: 27 July 2015
http://briwilliams.com.au/articles/Blog--News-How-can-it-go-so-wrong-when-research-says-its-right

Why you should ignore what customers say they want

If my previous life as a product manager taught me anything, it was to largely ignore what people told me they wanted.

It sounds arrogant I know, but it turns out that all of us - customers included - are really bad at predicting our own behaviour. As a business that means you can risk making the wrong decision based on what customers say they'll do rather than what they actually will.

We say we want serious stuff but end up consuming fluff

According to US journalist Derek Thomson there's a significant mismatch between what news people say they want to read and what they actually do, or as he puts it "Ask audiences what they want, and they'll tell you vegetables. Watch them quietly, and they'll mostly eat candy(121)."

For instance Americans claimed national, local, economic, political and international news were most important, but a review of the 'most read' articles suggested more interest in celebrity and human interest stories.

A spot check of Fairfax (The Age) and Murdoch (Herald Sun) online sites suggests Aussies are no different.

THE AGE	Herald Sun
Boy, 7, dies after getting buried in snow on Mount Buller **24K**	1. Ando's potential top 20 draft picks
OECD data shows ACT as best place to live **21K**	2. Family's frantic search ends in tragedy
	3. King still in ex-bikie's court
Why Robin Thicke appears a creepy stalker in Get Her Back video 20 **17K**	4. Super way to avoid going broke
	5. Karl puts everything on the line
	6. Recruiter defends dodgy Myer hire
Always five minutes late? Here's why **13K**	7. Watch Delta Goodrem's sexy strip
	8. Offspring's 'Nina' effect takes hold
Pharmacist suspects Stephen Dank forged his signature on peptide letter **11K**	9. Why I can't stop going to Bali
	10. THE LOOP: Melbourne's 100-storey skyscraper

Fairfax and Murdoch online news sites "Most Read" 26/6/14

This is a classic example of the "say vs. do" gap - the mismatch between what people think they want and what they actually use. People used to tell me they would use a list of rubbish bin days in their phone directory, but real behaviour sees those same people simply following whichever bin their neighbour has put on the kerb for collection.

The Say vs. Do Gap

The say vs. do gap stems from how humans think.

Most of the day we are on autopilot, relying on mental short cuts and rules of thumb to navigate the world. We typically use price as an indication of quality, for example. The upside is this helps us to make decisions efficiently; the downside is some of these decisions might be sub-optimal.

The interesting thing is that when someone asks what we might do we switch from our autopilot into our most considered, rational, thoughtful selves - the part we use only fleetingly during the course of an average day.

"Yes", we answer, "my health is important to me" before we go home and sit on the couch and eat ice cream. "Of course superannuation is important", we say before another year passes during which we've spent more time thinking about which day to buy petrol than our financial future.

Thankfully Behavioural Economics is a field of behavioural science that has not only uncovered the predictable biases in our decision making, but offers those of us in business a way of anticipating the responses of the 'auto pilot' version of the customer rather than the unrealistically rational 'pilot'.

Behavioural Economics gives you answers on how customers will actually behave

The diagram below illustrates how Behavioural Economics fills a gap in how we understand our customers (you've been introduced to this in Chapter 1). As a business we need to stake our decisions on two things:
1. Real rather than intended behaviour and
2. Future rather than past behaviour

Predicting behaviour

1. Real rather than intended behaviour

Many traditional mechanisms for understanding customer behaviour like focus groups or customer surveys rely on self-reports. In other words, we've been asking our customers to explain their behaviour. By doing so we've created a problem; engaging their pilot to explain autopilot behaviour. As we know, the 'say vs. do gap' makes this risky.

Behavioural Economics, on the other hand, relies on observed behaviour - what people actually do in response to a given set of circumstances. Rather than asking people why, Behavioural Economists focus on what. From 'the what' they then identify the bias underpinning the behavioural response which can then be applied to other contexts.

2. Future rather than past behaviour

In the absence of anything else, past behaviour can give you some indication of future likelihood. After all, people are creatures of habit and when in doubt will stick to the status quo.

But beware, this is a trap businesses fall into - we think because people have done something they will continue to. I know from painful experience that just because you've drawn a projection line in Excel doesn't mean the trend will happen! If you ever catch yourself thinking past behaviour will predict future with any accuracy, just remember Kodak, Blockbuster, Microsoft and 80's hairstyles.

So how do we get a sense of future behaviour if past behaviour might mislead?

Behavioural Economics identifies biases underpinning behaviour, and that means these principles can be used to anticipate, predict and shape future behaviour.

For example through the principle of Loss Aversion we know that people are more motivated to avoid loss than seek gain, so as a business we need to anticipate and shape our customer engagement strategy with this in mind. A barrier to take up of a new product or service is going to be that our customer may feel anxious about what they have to give up or that they have to trust a business they've never dealt with before, so we can develop a plan to mitigate this.

Should you really stop listening?

I know that ignoring what customers say seems extreme, and of course listening to feedback will help you understand how your customer has rationalised their experience with you. But always remember that the person you ask and the person who acts are likely to be different. A pilot's perspective is not necessarily the same as their autopilot's behaviour and as a business you need to understand who really holds the purchasing power.

Based on an article originally published: 27 June 2014
http://www.briwilliams.com.au/articles/Blog--News-Why-you-should-ignore-what-customers-say-they-want

Chapter 8. Pricing

When it comes to pricing, should you start high or low?

All businesses need to make a decision about how to communicate their prices. Is it better to start low and go high, or start high and go low?

Start low and go high

"Start low go high" is commonly used in car ads where a price is quoted like "$19,990 drive away" on the lowest model in the range to get people to the dealership. From there the real sales process begins, with upgrades to a better model and options like good 'ol car mats.

Real estate agents tend to use this strategy to get interested parties to the house, hoping that the prospective buyers will then become emotionally invested and stretch their budget (noting of course in Australia it is illegal for agents to under quote), and research has shown that lower starting prices can lead to higher final prices in auctions*(122)*.

Start high and go low

Most commonly used by service firms, the full 'bells and whistle' proposal is often quoted first which then allows the client and agency to negotiate around scope. The price can come down if the client can do without particular services. Restaurants and retailers can use this strategy to great effect to sell products that seem good value relative to the most expensive item; compared with the $99 lobster the $36 steak seems reasonable. At its worst, this strategy is used as an ambit claim by parties in negotiation, padding out their terms so it is easy to make subsequent concessions.

So which strategy is best?

Either can work, and both can fail. It all depends.

Starting low has the advantage of deferring 'sticker shock' until you have had a chance to engage the customer with your product. In the examples I've cited - car dealers and real estate agents - the businesses have trained sales people to manage the conversion process to transition the buyer from this initial emotional connection to becoming a paying customer.

Behaviourally the business is relying on both the customer's '**sunk cost**', where they have invested time, effort and/or money in the product and are therefore less willing to walk away, and the customer's '**mental accounting**' where they have already mentally 'spent' the lower amount on the product, and so feel that they only now have to pay for the incremental amount.

Research on auctions found that starting low resulted in higher prices due to not only the sunk cost and lower barriers to entry, but the '**herding effect**' of an item's popularity. In other words, when we see everyone else wants something, then we do too and are willing to bid more.

Starting high risks initial turn-off but has the advantage of landing on a mutually beneficial price where everyone feels like they've won. Central to this strategy is the behavioural principle of '**anchoring**' where we are most influenced by the first number we see. Just recall the last time you bought something on sale - you felt good because you knew how much the product used to cost - you were anchored to the Recommended Retail Price (RRP). Where starting low means the pricing news just gets worse for the customer as they consider options, anchoring them high allows them to feel better because the cost is decreasing.

How to know which strategy to use?

As frustrating as this is, it depends on your circumstance so I can't give you a directive here and now. What I will say is that you need to tune in to your customers and marketplace.

For online retailers who need to list their products, I would give serious consideration to sequencing your items from highest to lowest. However if you are an e-Bay seller who uses auctions, then starting low will fuel the feeding frenzy that should drive up the price. For professional service firms who typically need to talk about scope with clients, I would look at how you can use price anchoring, whereas firms who are dealing in a price sensitive, largely undifferentiated market where lead generation is key should consider low price products with which to entice customers.

Based on an article originally published: 20 January 2014
http://briwilliams.com.au/articles/Blog--News-When-it-comes-to-pricing-should-you-start-high-or-low

Should you use rounded or non-rounded pricing?

Imagine you are selling a brand of sparkling wine. Does it make a difference to your ability to sell if you price it at a nicely rounded $40.00 or a non-rounded $39.72? What if you were selling a calculator? Does rounding make a difference?

Researchers recently considered the issue of price rounding and its impact on customer intent*(123)*. Here are some of the key take outs.

Depends on product type

For products that are utilitarian (like calculators), customers tend to use cognition to assess their reaction whereas for products that are hedonic (like sparkling wine), they rely on emotion. Because customers like their purchase to 'feel right' to them, they seek a match between the way they think about it (i.e. cognitively or emotionally) and the way the number is represented. For cognitive products, non-rounded numbers work ($39.72) whereas for hedonic products, rounded is best ($40.00).

Depends on reason for purchase

The researchers wanted to know whether buying the same product (e.g. a camera) for a different reason made a difference to how prices were perceived. In one scenario participants were told the camera was for a family holiday (hedonic goal), and in another, for a school project (utilitarian goal). They found that when people were buying for a hedonic reason, the camera with a rounded 'feeling' number was perceived to take higher quality photos, whereas a non-rounded number evoked higher anticipated satisfaction amongst those considering a camera for a school project.

Depends on their thinking capacity

It's helpful to think of your customers as having two thinking systems; System 1 and System 2. As you've read throughout this book, System 1 is their emotional, impulsive, habitual, reactive thinking and System 2, their rational, cognitive, reflective and critical thinking. Most of the time we operate using System 1, saving our energy-sapping System 2 for more difficult situations.

The researchers wanted to know whether customers would react differently to prices if their System 2 was switched on or off. What they found was that when participants had to memorise 7 letters (occupying their System 2 and leaving no room for cognition), rounded numbers lead to stronger purchase intent for a pair of digital camera binoculars whereas memorising only 1 letter, and therefore having the capacity to think lead to non-rounded numbers being better.

Where to for your pricing strategy?

Where does this leave you with your pricing? Probably scratching your head because it is clearly a complex field. Overlay this research with work on price anchoring, priming and decimals and you have a lot of concepts to reconcile. The short answer is to be aware of research like this and to create an opportunity in your business to test variations. What happens when you round your prices? What about for only some product lines or for only some purchase occasions? Is it different for customers in a complex sale rather than a simple one?

Based on an article originally published: 14 November 2014
http://www.briwilliams.com.au/articles/Blog--News-Should-you-use-rounded-or-non-rounded-pricing

How to price to sell more quickly

Let's say you want to move some stock quickly. How do you let your customer know that you are open to negotiating? According to some recent research, it could be as easy rounding your price*(124)*.

How you list your price is as important as what the price actually is

One of the key decisions we have to make in business is how we should price our goods and services. Not only do we need to come up with a price point that we think the market will accept, we have to work out how to display the price.

Should we use decimals? Commas? Dollar signs? How big should the typeface be? What typeface should we use? What colour? Should the number be rounded or not?

As with most things, the devil is in the detail and sadly too many businesses are still relying on guesswork and intuition rather than science.

Signalling your eagerness to sell

Imagine you are an impatient seller listing on eBay. You are less interested in maximising the sales price and more interested in getting the stock sold. How can you signal your eagerness to sell? Are you better to list your price as $200 or $198? A rounded number or a precise number?

According to the study of over 10.5 million eBay "Best Offer" listings, rounded number listings:
  * received offers approximately 6 to 11 days sooner on average than precise-number listings and
  * were 3%-5% more likely to sell than precise-number listings.

However:

 * Rounded number listings attracted lower offers and sold at prices that were 5%-8% lower on average than nearby precise-number listings.

They also found that sellers who used a rounded number made less-aggressive counter offers and were more likely to settle with their customer whereas those who used precise numbers tended to stick to their guns and bargain more aggressively. In other words, it seemed the sellers using rounded numbers were much more ready to do a deal.

The researchers also analysed sales data from the real estate market and similarly found "round numbers are correlated with lower sale prices [which] suggests that round-number signalling is more a general feature of real-world bargaining". This lead the researchers to conclude that round numbers act as a signal to the buyer that the seller is looking to get the deal done. In their words, it's a "cheap-talk" signal.

Bringing some other research into the mix

You can take from this research that a rounded price in the context of a negotiation sends your customer the subconscious message that you are keen to sell. But that is not your only consideration when it comes to pricing.

For instance, whether to use rounded or precise numbers may depend on the type of product or service you sell.

As we've just read in the previous article, researchers investigating the impact of rounding found that for hedonic purchases (those that make you feel good like holidays and wine), rounded pricing (e.g. $40.00) did the better job of increasing purchase intent. For things that are utilitarian (insurance, buying a camera) however, non-rounded (e.g. $39.95) was more effective(125).

As we saw in Chapter 3, other researchers have delved into how people process numbers, and whether this is impacted by elements like decimals and commas*(126)*. Sure enough they found the inclusion of commas (e.g., $1,599 vs. $1599) or cents (e.g., $1599.85 vs. $1599) led people to perceive the number to be bigger. Why? It seems we spell the number out in our heads and equate more syllables with numerical magnitude.

And yet more research has found that the size of the typeface you use in your pricing can impact how it is perceived, concluding that if you want people to think the price is low, use a smaller print*(127)*.

Devil in the detail indeed.

Based on an article originally published: 20 July 2015
http://www.briwilliams.com.au/articles/Blog--News-To-sell-more-quickly-round-your-prices

Should you list your prices or keep them guessing?

I was reminded recently of an article I read about a jewellery store that chose not to display any of its prices. Customers would stop, see a piece they liked and enter the store where the assistant would then be in a position to 'sell' the value. Or so the theory goes.

This scenario came into play for me recently when I was selling my house. On the advice of my real estate agent we elected to not include a price range for buyers, banking on the proposition that those interested enough would come to the property, fall in love with it and then be sounded out about what they would be willing to pay

In behavioural terms, we are talking about the absence of a price anchor. In other words, not affixing people to a price point in the hope that emotion will encourage them to offer more than you were expecting.

This strategy appeals to those who want to 'control' the value assessment discussion rather than defend against a low pitch. However there are some risks with not listing your price.

1. People simply don't engage

I typically walk past jewellery shops that don't display pricing because I want to avoid the power imbalance between the shop assistant and me. I don't want to be embarrassed if the item I fancy is out of my range.

2. You create an information vacuum

If you don't provide pricing then customers will look for the nearest comparable item against which to estimate a price range, so you'd do well to anticipate what that might be.

In my case, a house very similar to mine had sold below expectation about six months prior. This caused an issue because people naturally used that price as a proxy for mine even though there were significant, albeit subtle, differences between the properties.

This lead to many prospective buyers being 'anchored' to the low value and meant my property was at risk of being passed in at auction. Thankfully my agent was able to overcome this during negotiations, but only because the eventual buyer had fallen in love with the house.

Next time around I would insist a price range be specified to avoid this anchoring-by-proxy problem.

3. You don't filter your customers

By not providing pricing cues the jewellery shop may well have had curious shoppers come in and talk with the assistant. But what good is that if they can't afford the item? You've just swallowed up precious staff time.

Likewise, attracting property buyers who are well out of range might generate a crowd on auction day but it's no good if they are priced out of bidding. This wastes everyone's time and is one of the pet irritations homebuyers have.

So should you list prices?

Your decision about whether to list prices and price ranges ultimately rests on your uniqueness in the market (i.e. whether and what will serve as proxy) and how you best want to use your sales staff.

This is how I would approach the decision about listing my price:
    * If I am the jewellery store I might not list all prices but I would certainly include a few to help people get a feel for the price range. (In fact this is

what I do on my website - I list some services but not others that require a briefing.)

* If I'm selling a house that has comparable properties that have sold well, I would not list a range because the market has created a favourable expectation amongst customers

* If I'm selling a house that has comparable properties that have not sold well, I would definitely include a range to signal my differentiation and make buyers curious about why mine is worth more

* If I am selling a house without comparable properties, I would either not list a range and leave the discussion to those who viewed the property, or - if I needed to filter out 'tyre kickers' - list a vague staring price that signalled that only offers above that range would be considered

Based on an article originally published: 9 February 2015
http://briwilliams.com.au/articles/Blog--News-Should-you-list-your-prices-or-keep-them-guessing

Pay What You Want Pricing

Imagine you are about to check out from your overnight stay at a hotel. You get to the counter and the receptionist smiles and asks "how much would you like to pay?"

Say what? A hotel where you can choose to pay what you want?

It's not a dream. It's happening right now in Paris where a group of hotels allow you to book one of their rooms and pay only what you think the stay was worth(128).

Is this risky business? Surely people will jump at the opportunity to short change the hotel, paying much less than the standard rate? After all, we all love getting stuff for free.

Well it's probably not as risky for the hotel as it first appears. Availability is limited to a set number of rooms and the interest the promotion has generated will probably outweigh any margin they lose on the standard rate. But more importantly, Behavioural Economics suggests that most guests will probably pay a fair amount anyway.

Where PWYW pricing is being used

As the name suggests, Pay What You Want (PWYW) pricing leaves it up to the customer to pay what they think the product/service is worth and has been trialled in a number of ways.

* Musicians like Radiohead and Amanda Palmer have released music that can be accessed for free but where payment is requested. Fans being fans, both have ended up making more money than they would have through traditional retail releases.

* Food outlets like Panera in the US provide access to food for those in need but end up being subsidised by those who can pay and who tend to pay more because they support the cause

* Museums like The Met in New York often request an entry donation

* The Freakonomics podcasters have requested that loyal listeners make a contribution to keep the show available for 'free'

PWYW pricing gambles on the promise that people will pay for something they find valuable. But when customers can get something they need for free, why on earth would they pay?

Social pressure

Whether we think so or not, we are influenced by what we see others do and by what we think they think about us. Social Norms mean we are more comfortable following what the normal thing to do is. This has an influence on PWYW in two ways.

1. We behave differently when we are being watched
A 2011 study tested whether being watched changed behaviour[129]. In this case people contributed more to an honesty box in the staff canteen when it was decorated with a picture of eyes rather than a picture of flowers. The subconscious sense of being watched was enough to change behaviour.

This suggests that a PWYW scheme can improve the likelihood of fair payment if the customer has to look you in the eye when deciding how to settle their account.

2. We do what others do
In the absence of explicit pricing, if we see other people paying a certain amount for a service we will be more likely to follow suit. No one likes looking cheap.

For a PWYW scheme it would therefore be helpful to provide "most people pay..." messages to help the customer come to a decision.

Frame of reference

Ask Australians to list their anxieties about visiting the US and one is sure to be tipping. Coming from a country where tips are relatively rare, Australians seek guidance as to what an adequate tip entails. 10%, doubling the tax, $1 per drink...these are the social rules that outsiders cling to so they don't insult the service provider.

In the case of the Parisian hotels, customers will at least be able to judge the price relative to what a normal room rate would be, so they are not without a price 'anchor' against which they can assess value. This is important because it will mean they are most likely to pay nearer the anchor price than they would have without any frame of reference.

In situations where no frame of reference is available however, it is likely that your customers will feel anxious about determining a fair price. This can result in under payment, over payment or worst of all, avoidance.

I am probably not alone in admitting that I steer clear of situations where I have to pay what I want because the anxiety about how I should value the service outweighs the experience. Pricing is something I would prefer not to burn mental and emotional energy on and I'd rather deal with a business whose pricing is unequivocal.

This is the risk that can be underestimated in PWYW businesses: avoidance due to Anxiety. How many people might you be turning off because they are too anxious about determining fair payment?

PWYW safe guards for your business

If you trial a PWYW system here are some suggested safe guards to make sure people pay:

   * Provide a reference for what is recommended - it will reduce Anxiety amongst your customers and increase the likelihood they will want to participate

* Consider using social cues like "most people pay..." to guide their decision

* Assume that you will attract some freeloaders, but that they will be offset by people who pay above your standard rate

* Customers who wish to return to your business will be more likely to pay so it may work best for businesses with repeat clientele

* Linking your offer to a charitable cause will encourage generosity(130)

* Make the payment process personal. Eyeball the customer rather than allow them to pay without any human interaction

PWYW pricing is a novel approach that depends very much on your ability to persuade customers to behave in a way you would prefer. It's not for the faint of heart but can set you apart from others in your market.

Based on an article originally published: 4 August 2014
http://www.briwilliams.com.au/articles/Blog--News-Why-Pay-What-You-Want-
Pricing-May-Not-Be-as-Crazy-as-it-Seems

Should you give away free stuff?

Every business gives away free stuff to a greater or lesser extent. Having a shop or website that people can browse is offering something for free.

Free is its own price point and can work because there's little downside for your customer in proceeding. This is particularly important if people have to get to know you or your product before they'll be ready to commit to a purchase (and is why I offer a free newsletter and copy of my book *"22 Minutes to a Better Business"*).

Unfortunately, it also means there's therefore nothing at stake for them, no 'skin in the game', and as such they can take it for granted.

Which is why it ends up being a question of conversion. A numbers game.
    * If you offer nothing for free then you have to make sure you are overcoming any resistance to your product or service using other strategies, like **Social Norms** and **Scarcity** because your field of prospects will likely be narrowed.
    * By offering something for free you are helping to fill your funnel, but your conversion tactics to convince people to buy have to be spot on because they are anchored at a price point of zero. Your efforts therefore have to be about differentiating the value of your free and paid offers.

Based on an article originally published: 24 June 2015
http://briwilliams.com.au/articles/Blog--News-Should-you-give-away-free-stuff

Should you offer free advice? Should you take it?

"Why are we more likely to follow advice when we have to pay for it?"

This was the question posed by a reader who was curious about why customers are more likely to change their behaviour (in this case wear a piece of protective attire) when they have to pay for it.

On a rational basis, it shouldn't make a difference. We seek advice from an authority and whether we pay or not should not matter to our subsequent behaviour.

But as anyone who has offered free tickets to an event only to find no one turns up knows, money changes things. Whenever I offer a mix of free and paid tickets to a webinar, for example, it is those who pay who are much more likely to attend.

So what's going on? A couple of things.

Money raises the stakes

When something is free there is no 'skin in the game'. The absence of outlay means there is little to lose by not participating.

When we pay for something on the other hand it means the stakes have been raised – we have something to lose if we don't participate. And thanks to Loss Aversion we know that we are strongly motivated to avoid suffering a loss, even more than we are motivated to seek a gain, which means walking away from something we've paid for is unpalatable.

In this sense money acts as a form of commitment device that locks us into a course of action that we may not otherwise follow.

We want to believe we make good decisions

Aside from the pain of wasting money by not adhering to the recommendation, the other factor at play is **Cognitive Dissonance**.

Cognitive Dissonance is the unpleasant feeling we have when our actions and beliefs are not consistent. In this case, if I have paid for advice I am more likely to follow it because I want my actions (paying for advice) and beliefs (that I'm a smart person who only pays for things of value) to be consistent. If I pay for advice but do not follow it I will have to reconcile the tension between my beliefs and actions, typically by disparaging the quality of the advice ("they didn't know what they were talking about") rather than my decision to seek it.

When are we less likely to follow advice? When it confronts us with something we don't want to do, even if it's the best thing to do. In behavioural terms, System 1 emotion overrides System 2 rationality and the result is a whole lot of rationalisation.

As a business should you ever offer free advice?

If you want people to change their behaviour and follow your advice, should you ever offer it for free? Of course! I do it in my blog every week. The trick is to define a level at which the stakes need to be raised.

If yours is a business that trades on your Intellectual Property and experience to some degree - and that's most of us, whether you're a builder, a financial planner, a cake decorator or a consultant – you have to offer a level of advice to gain trust and prove your credibility. But think of it as an entrée rather than the main course, whetting the appetite without satisfying it. That means, for example, giving enough information to the customer about protective attire that they feel anxious about not having it, but not giving them the attire for free.

Based on an article originally published: 20 April 2015
http://www.briwilliams.com.au/articles/Blog--News-Should-you-offer-free-advice-Should-you-take-it

Chapter 9. Acquisition

Conquering a fear of cold calling

It just doesn't come easily to me, calling people and interrupting their day. Whether it's my introverted nature or star sign, I have always had a mental block against cold calling - a problem when you are running a business and need to spread the word.

Pretty clearly I needed to change my behaviour. Putting aside "doctors make the worst patients and teachers the worst students" I became my very own case study of how to change behaviour. Here's how I did it.

Behaviour Change Model

To understand the behavioural barriers that were preventing me from moving from my current behaviour (i.e. not cold calling) to my desired behaviour (i.e. cold calling 6 businesses a week) I used the Williams Behaviour Change Model. The three barriers to address were Apathy, Paralysis and Anxiety.

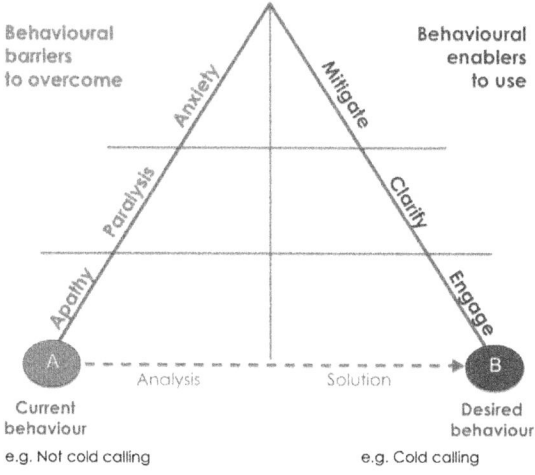

Barriers to cold calling

Apathy

Apathy is the way I talk about failing to recruit System 1- our intuitive, emotional, fast-thinking selves - to the cause. When we ask ourselves to do something we really don't like doing we'll find any excuse not to, and believe me I was finding lots of reasons not to make calls. Wrong time of day...school holidays...wrong day of the week...I'll feel like it tomorrow... I'm too busy...and because I'm my own boss I could easily excuse myself without fear of accountability.

Remember that any new behaviour is effortful - requiring System 2 processing - and we are geared to follow the path of least resistance and stick to existing habits. In other words, be "lazy". My task was therefore to make cold calling as easy as possible and find a way to keep myself accountable.

How I conquered Apathy

To make cold calling easy and hold myself to account I used four techniques:

1. **Write it down.** Two cold calls are added to my to-do list in my diary. The act of physically handwriting them made it harder for me to disregard (I find it too easy to ignore electronic alerts).

2. **Seinfeld Method.** Jerry Seinfeld writes a joke everyday and marks it with a big red cross on his calendar once it's done knowing that we are loath to break a chain of success. For me I mark off each week that I have met my goal.

3. **Normalising the task.** Part of my goal was to call across at least three days. Why? I'm trying to normalise the calls as part of my workday rather than a once-a-week binge.

4. **Public declaration.** Being true to my word is important to me so by writing this article I am holding myself up as someone who can and does cold call.

Paralysis

When we have too many options we can find it overwhelming and fail to act - the Paradox of Choice. In my case I was confronted with the question "Who should I call"? I started looking at online directories but found that this seemingly endless list didn't help me decide because all the businesses seemed equally weighted. My task was to limit and structure my options.

How I conquered Paralysis

The answer for me was to use a print phone directory because it helped in three ways;

1. The ads gave me more a feeling of the size of the organisation.
2. I could judge how many businesses were in the category.
3. I could mark off those I contacted as a record of my progress.

Anxiety

Loss Aversion, when the fear of what we stand to lose drowns out any appetite for gain is the biggest hurdle of the bunch, and for me it was an irrational fear of rejection.

Sure, intellectually I knew it wasn't personal but asking for help doesn't come easily. Fear of annoying someone, being asked a question I couldn't answer, or sounding stupid are deep seated (and irrational) anxieties that were preventing me from reaching out. I can happily talk to a room of 1,000 but making an unsolicited call to a stranger was my Achilles heel.

How I conquered fear

The more I cold call the less anxious I feel, but here's how I specifically dealt with fear:

 * **Shrunk the task:** Six cold calls may not seem like a lot to some people but the secret of habituating a new behaviour is to keep it really small so it doesn't seem daunting.

 * **Reframed:** "Cold calls" is a tainted label so I decided to reframe and instead refer to it as "Howdy calls", tricking myself into thinking that all I'm doing is saying hello. Not selling, not asking for commitment, just

introducing myself.

   * **Saw an expert in action:** One of my kind and talented friends invited me to watch and learn so I could see how harmless an exercise it was.

If you are reading this and just thinking, "What's the problem? Pick up the phone!" then this article is clearly not written for you, though I hope it has provided an insight into the battles many of us face. Where some people prefer to talk and be the focus, others prefer to listen and focus on others - neither is right or wrong and both come with their challenges. The good news is that any of us can change how we behave, and the Behaviour Change Model is a really great way to go about it.

Based on an article originally published: 4 May 2015
http://briwilliams.com.au/articles/Blog--News-How-I-overcame-my-fear-of-cold-calling

How to get your pitch perfect using Behavioural Economics

It was early in my consulting career and I was putting proposals together for the first time.

After reading my proposal a prospective client gave me some feedback that changed the course of what I do.

She said "You don't practise what you preach".

Ouch.

You see this client had loved my seminar on the application of Behavioural Economics to business, but when it came to my proposal, didn't see me demonstrating those same techniques.

And she was right. When it came to outlining my offer I had reverted to the same logic-driven, rational, boring pulp that any consultant could put forward.

I'd been so focused on using Behavioural Economics to influence her customers I'd forgotten to use it to influence her.

Sure, adopting the status quo method of putting a proposal together felt safe, but clearly wasn't the path to success.

And it's a mistake I see a lot amongst those who have to pitch for business - advertising agencies, research agencies, recruitment agencies included - service providers in the Business-to-Business (B2B) space who have to influence the decision-maker to buy their expertise.

They've assumed decision-makers are influenced by rationality when, just like consumers, the truth is decisions are reached through filters of cognitive and behavioural biases and heuristics. Just because your customer has a fancy title doesn't mean they are not subject to these same mental short-cuts.

In fact two-thirds of senior decision-makers who claim to be 'data or empirically driven' confess to trusting their intuition when it comes to making a decision*(131)*. When asked what they would do when data contradicted their gut feeling, 57% said they'd reanalyse the data and 30% would collect more. In other words, decision-makers decide first with their intuition (System 1), and then seek to support it with facts (System 2).

So what do I do differently as a result?

My proposals are now in a completely different format, written to engage System 1 'gut feel' while covering off System 2 detail. More specifically, I present my proposals as a story based on my understanding of the problem from the client's point of view, use a lot of visuals and break-outs to capture System 1 attention, mitigate points of negative tension (Loss Aversion) through anchored pricing, credibility and authority cues (Social Norms), while using positive tension (Loss Aversion again) to compel my client to proceed.

The same goes with pitches – for myself or when helping clients with their pitches I build a story like a three Act play using points of tension and resolution rather than a dull, unsurprising rational deck of slides. The result? It engages the customer and appeals to the part of them that actually makes the decision.

Tips for you

 * Humans are naturally receptive to stories, so construct your proposal with a beginning (the problem, the promise and what's at stake), middle (how the journey will unfold) and end (how you resolve it)
 * Ask your buyer to do you a small favour – it will make them think they like you more (**Reciprocity**)
 * Utilise positive tension and mitigate negative tension throughout your pitch
 * Dull Word documents that are all text will rarely interest the brain, and once System 1 is disengaged you've lost the game

* When it comes to pricing, contextualise, contextualise, contextualise. Don't just stick a number on a line by itself without talking about value.

Based on an article originally published: 25 May 2015
http://briwilliams.com.au/articles/Blog--News-How-to-get-your-pitch-perfect-using-behavioural-economics

Reducing the pain of paying

There's been some press lately on the move by Visa and MasterCard to eradicate signatures, meaning customers can only use their PIN to authorise a payment*(132)*.

The Reserve Bank of Australia seems persuaded by the argument that this will help to reduce card fraud, but I thought it would be interesting to turn attention to what it may do to customer behaviour.

Money hurts

Parting with hard-earned money is a psychologically painful experience for consumers. No matter how much they may want what they're buying, it still hurts.

Over the years and in order to make consumption more convenient, credit card and point of sale companies like Eftpos and PayPal have introduced technology to simplify transactions. Gone are the days of running a manual imprinting machine over the card, filling out details and dealing with triplicate copies. Now customers can wave their cards at a Point of Sale (POS) machine without even pausing to key a PIN.

For business, this is a good thing. Not only has the paperwork been reduced, but so too the pain of parting with money.

Separating the pain of paying from consumption

The transition from cash to signed card to PIN card to chip card to 'wave' card to... yes it's happening, micro chipping*(133)*, is separating the act of consumption from the pain of paying. In behavioural terms we are dealing with **"salience"**; how much the act of paying stands out in the mind of your customer.

The less it feels like you are paying for something, the less painful it will seem. Casinos know this all too well which is why they have customers gamble with chips rather than real cash.

Aside from the method of payment, strategies to reduce the pain of payment include:

   * Removing the dollar sign from menus: Dollar signs have been shown to trigger associations with money and reduce propensity to spend(134)

   * Subscription plans: While it can be tricky to get customers to pay upfront, once they do they are more prone to forget the cost of the service

   * Delayed invoicing: Ever noticed that Apple let you buy from iTunes but don't send you the 'painful' receipt immediately? Not only does this separate the consumption from the payment but they also cleverly aggregate separate purchases so their customers only get hit with pain once rather than multiple times. Oh yes, and it is also means less paperwork for the customer too.

For your business

The experience your customer has with you includes how and when you ask them to pay. It should be your objective to make this pain and hassle free. Not only seek to eliminate unnecessary steps and paperwork in the process, consider how best to schedule and communicate any request for payment.

Based on an article originally published: 21 October 2013
http://briwilliams.com.au/articles/Blog--News-Reducing-the-Pain-of-Payment--

Chapter 10. Retention

Four ways to retain customers

We've talked a lot about changing people's behaviour, but what if you want them to stay the same? Retaining customers for example?

The business case for prioritising retention is pretty clear. The Australian Communications and Media Authority (ACMA), for instance cited research that*(135):*

* Increasing retention by only 2% has the same effect on profits as having to cut costs by 10%

* Reducing defection by 5% can increase profits by as much as 125% and

* It costs 5-7x as much to acquire as retain customer

And yet retention – or churn – is a big issue in a lot of industries, particularly those with:
* Low engagement
* Price sensitivity and
* Undifferentiated offers

Customers leaving is unnatural

We humans are an inherently lazy bunch. By that I mean we are good at following the path of least resistance and, thanks to **Status Quo Bias**, leaving things as they are. Typically this inertia is something we have to work hard to disrupt in order to acquire customers and get them to take action.

So given inertia is the default, the fact that someone can be bothered to leave you is a BIG wake up call. It means that if we want to hold on to more customers we need to work out how we can impede their path to change and/or engage them to stay.

Impeding or engaging

Let's look at retention through the two ingredients of behaviour; motivation and ability(136).

Motivation is how customers are thinking and feeling about you and their alternatives, and ability is their capacity and capability to take action. For retention these elements form the basis of four key strategies.

Customer Retention Strategies

© Bri Williams People Patterns Pty Ltd

	Enable	Impede
Motivation What they think & feel *Hearts & minds*	1. Increase motivation to stay	2. Decrease motivation to leave
Ability What they do *Hands & feet*	3. Make it easy to stay	4. Make it difficult to leave

1. Increase motivation to stay

With an emphasis on making your customer feel like they want to stay, the best way to increase their motivation is to develop a relationship. Make it personal, addressing them by name not number and using collective pronouns ("we" and "us") to signal there are real people working for them. It's easier to break up with a business than a person, so try to lift the veil of anonymity to increase the stick-factor.

Of course you can also try rewarding them.

Extrinsic rewards such as discounts, vouchers and prizes are a classic way to increase motivation. Discounts for early renewal, for instance, can help to secure your customers before competitors have a chance to entice them with competing offers.

Another technique is to show them how close they are to attaining the next level of service or discount. This uses "**Completion Bias**" to motivate them to continue (e.g. pre-stamped coffee cards).

You can also try intrinsic rewards, which are about tapping into the customer's inherent desire to feel good about their choices ("a smart decision maker like you..."). This could also mean appealing to their need for **Consistency** – they've declared their desire to work with you before, so leaving would be recanting on their commitment.

2. Decrease motivation to leave

While at first sight decreasing motivation to leave might seem the same as increasing the motivation to stay (and in practical terms you can group them together), it's worth teasing out the nuance so we can understand the underpinning psychology.

While increasing motivation to stay is about giving them something to gain, decreasing motivation to leave is about making your customers feel they have something to lose.

Do you offer years of membership discounts like Victorian insurer RACV? Or loyalty points? Build something into the relationship that means there's something at stake if they leave. In behavioural terms, we're talking about **Loss Aversion** and **Sunk Cost** – we're loath to walk away from effort we've expended.

Goodness knows I renew my CPA membership every year because I can't stand the thought of losing my hard earned accreditation!

3. Increase ability to stay

Sometimes we make it difficult for customers to stay with us. Inflexible terms, difficult payment processing mechanisms, convoluted phone menus, and the absence of (communicated or real) value create points of friction in your renewal process. Such things increase the effort required by your customer, and leaves you exposed to churn.

Clear Calls to Action, dedicated phone numbers or web pages, straightforward invoicing, invoicing reminders, and pre-populated forms are all ways to make it easy.

4. Decrease ability to leave

Aside from the aforementioned Sunk Cost, you can make it complicated for customers to leave. I'm not necessarily advocating these strategies by the way, but the types of things some business do:
   * Make links to unsubscribe difficult from their email marketing campaigns
   * Force you to call (and wait on hold) rather than cancel online or by post
   * Introduce exit fees and penalties

One company that impressed me with this strategy was insurer Youi. In order to cancel my policy I had to call them and speak with one of their staff rather than do it online. Through that conversation they were able to win me back by bettering the competitor's price.

By pulling apart motivation and ability, and thinking in terms of enabling or impeding we can more easily anticipate and resolve weak points in our retention strategy.

Based on an article originally published: 16 November 2015
http://briwilliams.com.au/articles/Blog--News-Four-ways-to-hold-on-to-customers

Building better loyalty programs

Despite all the brains and bucks that go into loyalty programs, they are hard to get right and easy to get wrong if recent experience is anything to go by.

The latest to fail is supermarket retailer Woolworths' revamped Rewards loyalty program(137). The scheme, where customers accrue "Woolworths dollars" to use in a future shopping occasion by purchasing selected items, has apparently left customers underwhelmed.

Not that rival Coles can laugh after its "My5" debacle only a few years ago which gave customers a 10% discount on five favourite items(138). Pulled from market faster than a Dawn French punch line, Coles learnt that too much effort for too little reward equals customer inertia.

I'm going to leave for another time the debate about whether loyalty programs are ever worthwhile, and why I believe it's more important to focus on building habits rather than 'loyalty', and instead share some of the behavioural principles you'll need to consider if you are keen on developing a system of rewarding your customers.

Think of this like a pantry list rather than recipe because not everything should be used to cook up an effective program.

Exclusivity

What: Limiting access to a loyalty program or making inclusion subject to strict criteria.

Upside: Member only benefits can appeal to the ego of your customer and give others something to aspire to. The membership is a form of social currency. At the extreme, you could make your program by invitation only, using scarcity to drive perceived value.

Downside: You limit your market and risk disenfranchising potential customers.

Example: AMEX's Black Card, by invitation only

Flying start

What: Thanks to **Completion Bias** we know that people are more likely to persevere with your program if they are given a flying start.

Upside: Low cost and high reciprocity factor when your customer feels you are doing something nice for them.

Downside: You take a small hit by advancing them points and it can be taken for granted by the customer if you don't make it seem like a special thing you are doing just for them.

Example: Stamping a coffee card with 2 coffees for a new customer works since they feel like they are closer to their freebie.

Immediate gratification

What: Discounts and bonus gifts experienced at the time of transaction.

Upside: Customers love benefits they can enjoy now.

Downside: Will the memory of the benefit be enough to bring them back to you?

Examples: Supermarket IGA where some products are discounted for their Community Benefit Card members. As an everyday low price environment, Aldi doesn't offer a 'loyalty program' as such, but they are using immediate gratification to very effectively build a shopping habit.

Intermittent rewards

What: Pokies are addictive in large part because they use intermittent rewards – you are never quite sure when you'll hit the jackpot. This can work with loyalty programs too by varying the timing of the reward.

Upside: Surprising the customer with their reward makes it more salient, plus it is disconnected from the pain of paying.

Downside: The reward can be so disconnected from the activity that it fails to build a relationship. Customers lose sight of what they are building towards.

Example: Retailer Myer's Myer One Program accrues points and then sends a $20 gift voucher to the customer, encouraging them to revisit the store with their 'free' money.

Something to lose

What: Thanks to the **Endowment Effect** we know that customers hate to walk away from benefits they have accrued.

Upside: This means that once they have points they will be loath to let them lapse.

Downside: The promise of rewards that pay off way down the track is rarely enough to convince people to engage in the first place. You therefore need to consider having realistic milestones between purchase and reward, and remind your customers regularly of what they have in their rewards 'bank'.

Examples: Watch George Clooney's "Up in the Air" if you want to see the lengths to which some customers will go to retain airline status points. Insurer RACV try this with their 'years of membership benefits' to retain customers.

Currency or points

What: Dollars are unambiguous whereas points can have assigned meaning.

Upside: Using points rather than dollars can increase the program's perceived value because the customer feels they are earning more than actually costs the business. On the other hand, dollars are easy to understand which could be enticing if yours is a generous program.

Downside: If the points are hard to understand or redeem for real value there is a chance the customer will forget all about them. If dollars are not significant your program will look stingy.

Examples: Airline points are so mysterious that customers never really calculate the real cost of spending to accrue them. Discount petrol vouchers use currency (4c off a litre) but shift the context - $3 off your grocery bill would be underwhelming, but 4 cents off 139 cents/litre seems more generous.

Based on an article originally published: 18 April 2016
http://briwilliams.com.au/articles/Blog--News-Building-better-loyalty-programs

Loyalty program campaigns: How to motivate customers to take action

Imagine you are part way through a task. Will you be more motivated to complete the task if I tell you are 67% through, or you have 33% to go? This question came to mind when I received this prompt from a loyalty program.

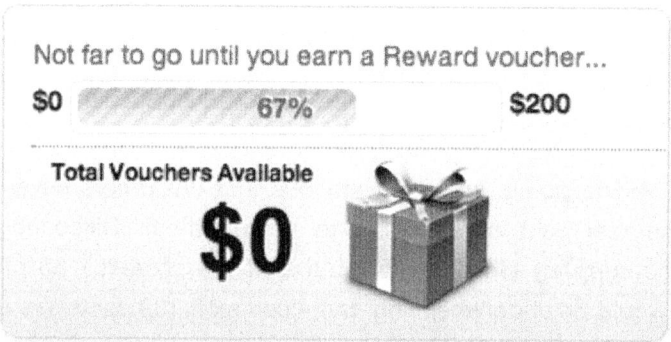

It's a pretty effective way of spurring the customer on towards their next Reward Voucher isn't it?

It taps into what's known as **"Completion Bias"** (or the **"Endowed Progress Effect"**), which is our tendency show greater persistence in attaining a goal once when we perceive we have progressed towards completion. So far, so good. Lesson one is that we like to see progress.

Progress completed vs. progress remaining

But here's the big question - what progress should you show? Is 67% completed better than 33% to go?

These are the challenges we are faced with all the time in business – having to make seemingly trivial decisions about how to write or design something without realising that they can make or break our effectiveness.

I refer to them as micro-moments and it's what, for me, behavioural science is all about. Providing answers so you don't have to guess.

Speaking of answers, the **"small-area hypothesis"** tells us that people are more motivated towards their goal if their attention is directed to the smaller representation of progress*(139).*

As small-area hypothesis researchers state:

> *"at the beginning of goal pursuit, directing attention to accumulated progress increases goal adherence relative to directing attention to remaining progress (e.g., 20% completed is more impactful than 80% remaining). However, with closeness to the goal, directing attention to accumulated progress lessens goal adherence relative to directing attention to remaining progress (e.g., 20% remaining is more impactful than 80% completed)."*

In other words, while the loyalty program had the right idea they would have been even more effective if they'd directed my attention to the 33% I had to go rather than the 67% I had already achieved. Conversely for customers who were just getting started, the focus should be on their progress to date (e.g. you're already 25% to your reward).

Based on an article originally published: 27 April 2015
http://briwilliams.com.au/articles/Blog--News-Loyalty-program-campaigns-How-to-motivate-customers-to-take-action

Chapter 11. Website Design

Creating a Behaviourally Effective Website

Whenever I talk to people about their websites there seems to be a sense of passive victimhood, a malaise about 2-5% conversion rates[140]. We search for benchmark performance and sigh with relief that our website is around average. Well guess what? Average is pathetic.

Imagine you had a corner shop and 100 customers came through your doors. Now imagine that 95 leave without buying anything. Horrifying isn't it? Pretty soon you'd be out of business. Then why do we accept that websites should only convince 5% of visitors to become customers?

I think it's because websites have been the domain of IT and as business owners or marketers we have been too hands-off. Even if it's something we have commissioned and paid for we have left the technicalities of how the site performs to others. To me that's like leaving the driving to your mechanic.

Stop thinking of websites as technical - it's about influencing human behaviour

Beneath it all I believe it's because we have trapped ourselves into thinking of websites as something technical when really, websites are just about changing the behaviour of your customer. Changing them from browsing to buying, from reading to clicking, from researching to transacting.

I say 'just', but changing someone's behaviour is one of the hardest things you can do and most websites do not do it effectively. That's why conversion rates are so low.

So what makes a website behaviourally effective? It influences your visitor to do what you want them to do in the most efficient manner for both parties, and that means you convert as many visitors as possible. In the following pages I'll be taking you step by step through the five things you should be doing to improve your website's Return On Ivestment (ROI) using behavioural science.

5 Essentials for a Behaviourally Effective Website

Essential #1: Establishing Confidence

You have somewhere between 0.5 and 7 seconds to convince your website visitor to stay on your site*(141)*. The first thing you need to lock in is "confidence", so let's look at how.

Confidence in Me

'Confidence in Me' is all about reassuring your visitor that they have arrived at their intended destination. Fail to do this and they'll click back to where they came from and you risk them never returning.

When someone lands on your website they have created an expectation in their mind about it. If they've clicked through from an ad, they will be looking for language and imagery that confirms that they have arrived at the right destination - this makes Landing Pages an ideal strategy because you have the freedom to tailor the page so that it mirrors the ad.

Unfortunately too many businesses are linking ads to their home page and expecting their visitor to make the content connection. Remember that your website's content is not familiar to your visitor and if you dump them on your site without helping to reassure that they are in the right place then you'll end up being dumped yourself.

Confidence in You

'Confidence in You' is about communicating your authority and credentials to your visitor. Who are you and are you worth getting to know? Remember this is all within a few seconds so it does not mean bleating about your history and philosophy - this is about industry accreditations, testimonials, years established, awards - anything that at a quick glance conveys that you are reputable.

Essential #2: Communicating Value

When it comes to communicating value, it's about the problem, not about you.

Imagine you're on a date and the person you are with blabs on and on about themselves. Pretty soon you lose interest. That's how many websites present themselves to their prospective customers - they talk about how great they are, their philosophy and how they give to charity. This might be great information to share, but not yet.

The most important thing to do before you talk about 'why you' is answer "What problem is my visitor looking to solve?" This is an essential and neglected step in winning your visitor's business because it connects your offer to the problem they are looking to solve. You are proving that you are on their wavelength. It is also the hardest step of the website essentials to

get right.

Four components of communicating value

There are 4 components of a communicating value:
1. Articulate the problem your visitor has,
2. Explain how you solve this problem,
3. Describe the payoff (What's In It For Me), and
4. Explain why only you can do this (unique differentiation)

Survey Monkey do a brilliant job of communicating value to their visitors, understanding that people do surveys to get answers. They step out the process (Design, Collect, Analyse) and write from the perspective of their customer - "Build your own...". What they don't do is clarify why only they can do this - their unique differentiation is missing.

Contrast this with another online survey software provider I visited. Here their copy is written in bragging style "There's a reason why our customers think we are the best survey tool" which doesn't speak to the problem their visitors have - looking for a way to get feedback - and is not written from the visitor's perspective.

Pod Legal are taking a fresh approach to legal services, and their proposition is "We do fixed fee billing", tapping into a problem their market has faced with fees. While the copy is written from the perspective of Pod Legal ("We do...") it works because it gets to the heart of the visitor's concern and is refreshing in it's bluntness. It clearly invokes their unique differentiation by inferring that others do not stick to their quotes. In behavioural terms they are using **Loss Aversion** to create Anxiety in the visitor about risking their money by using a different law firm.

This type of positioning also shows a level of courage - Pod Legal are banking on their target market being more concerned about fees than what types of legal issues are handled. For me this raises a question as to whether this proposition can remain sufficiently differentiated and whether they will need to draw on more of their points of difference to counteract competitors who can match their fixed fee promise.

From the outside in

To communicate value put yourself in the position of your ideal customer performing a search. Look at your website from the outside, in. Does it communicate your understanding of that problem and why you can solve it, or does it assume that people visiting the site will make the leap? Remember, just like on a date it's less about you, more about them. Make them feel like you're the only one for them.

Essential #3: Creating a Pathway

Click here! No, click here! Over here, buy now! Ignore them, click here!

If most websites could talk it would sound a bit like walking down Lygon Street in Melbourne where all the restaurateurs tout for your custom by waving their arms and yelling out their specials.

In website-land the equivalent is creating multiple competing pathways for your visitor to take and making them choose. Homepages with 4, 6, 16 different Calls to Action (CTAs), social media buttons taking prime real-estate and shopping-cart pages that distract the customer with newsletter sign-ups right at the point they should be focussed on completing the payment are all symptoms of your website's pathway being broken. And when it's broken you are leaking money.

Pathway to purchase

No doubt you've heard of path to purchase: the steps people take from researching their needs to finally buying the product or service. Knowing about the pathway is one thing, designing one for your business, and more specifically your website is another.

For every point at which you are asking your visitor to take an action (read more, click here, subscribe, download, buy), you must have already answered:
   * Where is this leading for the visitor and
   * Where is this leading for you?

Creating a pathway for the visitor

For the visitor the experience on your site needs to follow a logical progression. Don't ask me to buy from you before you've introduced yourself (Established Confidence), convinced me that you know about my problem (Communicated Value) and provided the information I need at the level and sequence that makes sense for me (Creating a Pathway).

Likewise when I'm at the checkout ready to buy, don't tell me about irrelevant services or worse, make it difficult to pay (e.g. insist on registering rather than allow me to buy as a guest).

Creating a pathway for you

For you, the discipline is in knowing how each touch point with a customer ultimately leads to a sale. If you have a newsletter, what role is it playing in building towards the reader wanting to do business with you? If you want people to leave your site to visit your Facebook page, how will you loop them back to be closer to doing business with you?

Traps to avoid when creating a pathway

Websites get their purchase pathways wrong for two reasons:
    * Greed - trying to sell everything to everyone and
    * Anxiety - being scared that if you don't provide everything at once then the visitor will leave

Both these reasons stem from a lack of confidence in your offer. As businesses we get terrified that if we don't have our phone number on the home page then the person who wants to contact us won't bother. Seriously? If you've convinced people of your value let me assure you that they will take the time to click on your "Contact Us" tab. In the meantime, by reducing the amount of content you are asking them to process on the home page (like removing superfluous and distracting Calls To Action (CTA), phone numbers and social media buttons) you are actually able to more clearly and calmly communicate your value. Have the discipline to hold back on anything that does not take you closer to the sale.

If you are interested in who does a pathway well, check out www.mailchimp.com for how to upgrade users from free to paid and www.amazon.com and www.pinterest.com for how to 'on-board' customers by taking them through a process of customisation.

Essential #4: Asking for Action

Imagine you have strolled into a homewares shop in your local neighbourhood for the first time. You are about to start doing a lap around the shop when the shop assistant steps in front of you and asks "So, do you want to buy now?". "Ahh, no I've just arrived." Awkwardly you slink past them and pick up a candle to look at. "So, do you want to buy now?" they ask. By this stage you are getting angry and feeling harassed, so you slap down the candle and leave the shop as soon as possible.

We know that coming on too strong in a shop is a sure fire way of botching the sale, so why do we do it online?

Four mistakes to avoid when asking for action

There are four common mistakes when asking your visitors to take action.

1. Absent Call to Action

A surprising number of websites don't include a Call to Action (CTA) on every page, forcing the visitor to leave the page that had convinced them to proceed and instead click around the rest of the website in the hope of working out what to do.

2. Unclear Call to Action

When a Call to Action doesn't explain what happens when the visitor proceeds, it will create Anxiety and reduce chances that they will go ahead. One example from a professional speaker/author's website asks the visitor to "Grab your copies today" but does not provide any information as to whether "grab" means to buy, order, or download for free.

Contrast this with an example from the author Michael Port who asks his visitors to "Click here to get 4 free chapters now". The visitor knows exactly what they will get if they add their name, email and click the button.

3. Too many Calls to Action

In our desire to help we can fall into the trap of providing multiple avenues for the visitor to pursue. The problem is that we can overload them and they will instead do nothing. Paralysis, the '**paradox of choice**', means people crave the freedom to choose but then get stuck trying to weigh options and worrying about whether they've made the right decision. Remember, less choice can mean more choosing.

4. Undifferentiated Calls to Action

Calls to Action that look the same as each other or the same as other elements on the website risk being overlooked by your visitor. A common mistake is to have the primary CTA button on the home page in the same colour as the logo and branding. While it might look pretty, it doesn't help to grab the visitor's attention and cue them that it is the most important thing to do on the page. Instead opt for contrasting but complementary colours.

Asking for the right behaviour in the right way

Here's the rule with Calls to Action; explain what the customer gets by doing what you ask. Sounds simple right? Then why are so many buttons labelled "submit" or "send"?

Essential #5: The Effort vs. Reward Equation

Let's bring behaviourally effective websites together with the essential that underpins all the others.

The Effort vs. Reward Equation that we read about in Chapter 3 is a pretty simple construct and its beauty is that you can apply it to any behaviourally situation - online or offline. Simply put when Effort is greater than the Reward, people won't do what you want the to. When Reward is greater than Effort, then you're in business! But if it's so easy, why do we get it so wrong? Three reasons.

1. Fixate on reward when effort is more important

According to Stanford University's BJ Fogg there are three things you need in order to make behaviour happen*(142)*:
* * Motivation: The desire to do something
* * Ability: The capability to do something and
* * Trigger: To be asked to do something

BJ's very elegant behaviour change model describes how Motivation and Ability are a trade-off. In other words, to get someone to do something really hard (a.k.a. effort), they have to be extremely motivated. Learning to drive a car is an example.

On the flipside, if something is easy to do then they don't really have to be motivated very much at all. New 'touch and go' payment terminals are an example of reducing the effort so that people don't use cash or other cards instead.

Most businesses spend a lot of their time focussing on the reward for their visitor (the motivational side) rather than simply making it easier to do business with them. And guess what? It's much harder to change your visitor's motivational state than it is to change how you let them take action with you. Marketers take note! Stop trying to win hearts and minds when you really should be concentrating on hands and feet to maximise ROI.

The good news is that by making your website easy to understand, navigate and interact with you will be able to convert more customers without having to entice them with fancy deals and discounts.

2. Forget that effort includes more than money

Effort includes more than money and that's why I call this the "Effort vs. Reward" equation rather than "Cost vs. Benefit".

Effort includes three components:

* Psychological effort - what my colleagues or friends will think about my decision; how anxious I feel about what you are asking me to do; how smart or stupid I feel trying to use your website

* Physical effort - how far my eyes have to travel across the page; how easy or difficult the fonts are to read; how many clicks I have to go through; how much data entry is required

* Economic effort - what it costs in my time as well as money

3. Think it's enough for effort to be equal to reward

Effort is associated with the behavioural principle of Loss Aversion where we are more motivated to avoid loss than seek gain. The magnitude of difference is about 1.5-2.5 times, so the payoff needs to be double the amount of effort.

The key here is to remember that whenever your visitor is looking to do something with you it means they have to give something else up. To commit to a new insurer, for example, I have to give up my familiarity with dealing with the old one. Same for banks. In fact why most of us stay with incumbent businesses is not because there aren't better offers out there, it's because we can't be bothered giving up the comfort of our status quo.

5 Essentials conclusion

I hope this overview of the 5 essentials for a behaviourally effective website has been helpful. Work through each essential and ask yourself how your website stacks up, or get me or your web specialist to do an appraisal. Websites are far too important to your results to rely on opinion-based design when behavioural science is available right now for you to use.

167

Based on articles originally published as follows;

15 April 2013
http://briwilliams.com.au/articles/Blog--News-Behaviourally-effective-websites-part-1-Establishing-Confidence--

22 April 2013
http://www.briwilliams.com.au/articles/Blog--News-Behaviourally-effective-websites-Part-2-Communicating-Value

29 April 2013
http://www.briwilliams.com.au/articles/Blog--News-Behaviourally-Effective-Websites-Part-3-Creating-a-Pathway

6 May 2013
http://www.briwilliams.com.au/articles/Blog--News-Behaviourally-Effective-Websites-Part-4-Asking-for-Action

13 May 2013
http://www.briwilliams.com.au/articles/Blog--News-Behaviourally-Effective-Websites-part-5-The-Effort-Reward-Equation

Chapter 12. People Management

Why job interviews are a waste of time

Years ago I heard someone suggest that to get to know a candidate, conduct the job interview while they drive you around the block. It sounded crazy, which is why it stuck in my mind.

So I was amused to see an interview with CEO Ron Kaplan in the New York Times where he said "I hand them my car keys and say, "Why don't you drive," and see what kind of reaction they have to driving my car in a strange city. Then I'll be giving them directions and asking them questions while we're driving to see if they can multitask. Some people can handle it with aplomb, and others can't*(143)*."

Let's look at why Ron is on to something, and how reaching for the keys could resolve the big flaw in job interviews.

The problem with job interviews

Job interviews are a necessary evil. We need to get to know the candidate, and they us. But do we actually get to know them?

In an effort to predict how the candidate will behave in the workplace, multiple formats of interview have been tried. Two of the most popular have been:
   * the behavioural interview – asking the candidate to tell you about a time when they have done something, and
   * the situational interview – asking the candidate to imagine what they would do in a situation.

Theory goes that in a behavioural interview, demonstrating a past behavioural competence will mean the candidate is more likely to demonstrate this behaviour in future. In a situational interview, being able to tell you what they will do will make them more likely to do so.

Both have a significant flaw.

You're hiring the Elephant, not the Rider

The flaw here, is that whenever you ask a candidate a question in an interview setting, you are getting an answer from the candidate's "System 2", rationalising, deliberative brain (a.k.a. The Rider), where you are really hiring their "System 1", habitual, fast-thinking, intuitive brain (a.k.a. The Elephant).

As we heard in Chapter 3, System 1 is what customers use day in, day out to navigate the bulk of their life and their work. With a massive processing capacity, the equivalent of 11,000,000 bits per second, the Elephant is what you end up working with most of the time.

System 2 is what people use for special occasions; situations that are unfamiliar, unusual or serious – you know, just like job interviews. System 2 is used only intermittently and can be depleted easily because its capacity, in contrast to System 1, is a mere 40-50 bits per second.

This explains why your job candidate will likely be exhausted after an interview – they've chewed up all their System 2 battery by trying to put on their best face. But it doesn't help you make a determination about who you are really employing.

Getting them to drive you around the block

Now imagine you are interviewing a candidate for a job. You've thrown them the car keys and you are on your way. They're in an unfamiliar car, driving on unfamiliar roads with an unfamiliar person beside them. What's happening to their brain?

Their System 2 has taken the wheel because, in this circumstance, the uniqueness of the situation demands heightened focus. Not crashing is their priority.

What happens when System 2's limited capacity is occupied? System 1 attends to lower-grade issues, like the questions you are asking them.

This means they are incapable of exerting the self-control (a System 2 function) that they normally would in answering the questions. They are less guarded and more intuitive. Whether this is a good thing is something you will judge, but at least you are meeting their Elephant not just the Rider.

So while Ron employs the driving technique to gauge his candidate's ability to multi-task and deal with unusual circumstances, he's actually giving himself an opportunity to get beneath the veneer we tend to present in highly artificial, traditional job interviews too.

Based on an article originally published: 14 September 2015
http://briwilliams.com.au/articles/Blog--News-Why-job-interviews-are-a-waste-of-time

Show me the money? Not if you want to drive performance

As a sports agent who was struggling to retain his last client, Tom Cruise in the movie Jerry Maguire was famously required to scream "Show Me the Money" to player Rod Tidwell to prove his dedication.

And while politeness usually prevents us from yelling those same words at whomever is asking us to do something for them, money has long been held up as a key motivating factor.

For good reason.

If we do not feel fairly remunerated or cannot support ourselves financially, then our motivation to perform will be low.

But once those factors are taken care of, once we feel we are getting a fair deal and our basic needs for shelter, food and security are covered does money really drive performance?

Apparently not.

In fact, the surprising conclusion from behavioural science is that money isn't that great at motivating behaviour.

Say what?

Money isn't a great motivator.

I can hear the ears of CFOs pricking up everywhere.

Here are some of my favourite, somewhat confounding, findings related to money in the workplace.

Non-monetary gifts are better at increasing performance

Researchers from the University of Zurich were interested in whether giving a monetary or non-monetary gift to employees was a better way to increase performance(144). Study participants who were given a cash reward of 7 euros increased performance by 5%. Not bad. But.

Study participants who were given a gift of the equivalent value (a thermos worth 7 euros) increased by 25%!

Money can make us selfish

Across a number of experiments researchers were interested in whether participants **primed** with money behaved differently to those who weren't(145). The priming was subtle. In one task, for instance, participants had to unjumble sentences (e.g., "high a salary desk paying" became "a high paying desk salary"), and in another, a stack of monopoly money was left in the peripheral vision of participants as they completed an unrelated task.

The researchers found that people primed with money were:
   * More self-reliant (asked for help less and chose to work alone)
   * Less willing to help others
   * More physically distant

Reminders of money seem to change the game, turning people inwards rather than outwards, which obviously has ramifications for any team based organisation.

We think we're motivated by money, but it can actually impair performance

We think we want cash. Remember the Zurich study into non-monetary gifts? One of the confounding findings was that when participants were offered a choice between cash and a gift, 80% said they preferred money.

A University of Chicago study similarly found that although performance was greater when subjects were treated with a massage rather than money, two thirds of people stated they would have preferred the cash(146). So when asked what would motivate us, it seems we are under the impression that cash is king. It's tangible, flexible and measurable.

But *money can impair our performance.*

In fact the London School of Economics has found that "financial incentives may indeed reduce intrinsic motivation and diminish ethical or other reasons for complying with workplace social norms such as fairness. As a consequence, the provision of incentives can result in a negative impact on overall performance(147)".

Going further, researchers found that while money was good for motivating routine, mechanical tasks (like pressing a key on a key board), it reduced performance for cognitive tasks (like an adding task)(148).

Cash may be king, but it's a scary ruler who makes us selfish and inhibited.

Monetary compensation in your workplace

So where does that leave us when it comes to monetary compensation in the workplace?
   * Money is your ticket to play – pay people poorly and they'll be so focussed on money that their performance and satisfaction will suffer
   * Reminders of money shift people from collective to individualistic goals – a problem if you rely on team work - and can compromise ethics and sense of fairness
   * Monetary rewards increase pressure and impair cognitive and creative thinking, and doesn't most of today's work require just those skills?
   * People might say they prefer money but non-monetary gifts are better at stimulating reciprocity

Based on an article originally published: 19 October 2015
http://briwilliams.com.au/articles/Blog--News-Show-me-the-money-Not-if-you-
want-to-drive-performance

Brilliant or crazy to offer unlimited annual leave?

One of the struggles many businesses have is how much freedom to give their employees.

In a perfect world people should just turn up, do a great job for a fair amount of pay and get on with things. They should be responsible, committed and able to work unsupervised.

But that's not always the case.

The reaction in many businesses is to clamp down and create ever more constraining policies. Policies for annual leave, sick leave, IT, hours of work, dress code, social media...the list is endless. The theory goes that if people know the rules they can be held to them.

The problem with this approach is that it turns an adult-to-adult relationship into something more like adult-to-child.

Instead of an employee being responsible for themselves, you take over this role and suffocate any chance of autonomy.

That's why I was so pleased to see a business owner trying something different. In the spirit of Netflix and Richard Branson, camera App start-up firm Triggertrap's CEO took a deep breath and launched an unlimited annual leave policy, having "decided that the act of actually tracking holidays was more hassle than it was worth *(149)*".

But then it backfired.

In the UK employees are entitled to 28 days leave which expire if they are not taken in the year. With the new policy, staff could take far more days than this, exposing the business to a labour shortage.

But that's not what happened.

Rather than people taking too much leave they didn't take enough.

Not one employee took their entitled 28 days, leaving the team fatigued at the end of a very busy year (Average 1.25 days/month).

Why people didn't take leave

According to Triggertrap two problems seemed to underpin people's reluctance to take leave:
   * Their entitlement was no longer on their pay slip so they weren't reminded of it and
   * People felt guilty taking days off because it no longer felt like it was theirs to use

It's counter intuitive, isn't it? You imagine that once given a 'blank cheque', staff will take as much as they can get away with. And occasionally this might occur.

But that's not how we are wired.

We are wired to:
   * largely conform with those around us. If no one in my team is taking leave then I won't either. (**Social Norms**)
   * mentally account for things like annual leave. When no limit is set there is no credit in the account to draw upon. (**Mental Accounting**)
   * pay attention to things that are top of mind. If annual leave is not brought to our attention we will get caught up with other things.
(**Availability Bias**)
   * prioritise now over later. Work can always seem busy in the moment so it is very hard to imagine taking time off. (**Short-Term Bias**)

* be paralysed by choice. Having to decide how many days to take from an unlimited number can perversely make it harder because it's difficult to know how much leave is 'right'. (**Paradox of Choice**)

As Triggertrap's policy experiment has shown, people's behaviour can surprise us. Where we might jump to the economic conclusion that employees will always seek to maximise their outcomes, the truth is that all behaviour is a function of a broader psychological context, and one that Behavioural Economics seeks to define for us.

How have Triggertrap resolved their policy?

The easy thing would have been to revert to the old adult-child system of tracking and capping leave. Instead Triggertrap have refined their approach, by:
   * paying a small cash bonus for taking at least 14 days within 6 months,
   * tracking days taken publicly so people are acknowledged for taking time off and it becomes the norm
   * encouraging team members to suggest team mates take time off because it's a good and healthy thing,
   * asking people to gain the consent of their team before they take leave, reducing people's sense of guilt about leaving team mates in the lurch.

The result? Since tweaking their policy every staff member has taken at least 10 days in 6 months (Average 1.8 days per month), which is heading in the right direction.

Above all else what I love most about Triggertrap is how they are willing to think differently about their relationship with employees, treating them as adults in the hope that it will ultimately lead to better outcomes for all.

Based on an article originally published: 10 August 2015
http://briwilliams.com.au/articles/Blog--News-Brilliant-or-crazy-to-offer-unlimited-annual-leave

Why training falls over

I sat in a seminar recently on team development and it prompted me to think about how Behavioural Economics can be used to improve team performance.

The presenter started by sharing the characteristics of high performance teams, citing the 2012 Australian Rules Football League premiers the Sydney Swans as an example. What elements of team dynamics were called out? Process, shared vision and values, playing for each other, clarity about the contribution each individual was expected to make and so on. People in the room had no trouble listing these elements, and yet we seem collectively to struggle on a day-to-day, hour by hour, decision by decision basis to make it happen.

Perhaps I'm jaded, but there seems to be an intractable disconnect between high performance teams and the rest of the world. For every Sydney Swans there is a lowly Essendon*. Where the Swans are the exception, the rest of us are the rule. And in spite of team dynamics being one of the most studied and trained aspects of organisational performance, an area we spend a fortune on, we scratch our heads and mutter "if only".

So what's breaking down?

Insights are fleeting, behaviour is entrenched

There's no doubt that team profiling tools and team-building sessions can improve performance. It's the sustainability of that performance that is at issue.

In a previous life when I facilitated induction days and team building events, and in other sessions in which I've participated, I've seen light bulbs go off. People gain insights into their colleagues and the walls get broken down between right brainers and left, between introverts and extroverts, between instigators and concluders. The team members see why they approach issues from a particular perspective and with that, develop an understanding of how their colleagues may see things differently. Finally! We have a shared understanding and common language that means 'conflict' is not necessarily personal, it's simply a function of us not being empathetic. Hurrah, at last we can be a high performance team!

But then something happens.

It's called habit. We revert to old patterns of behaviour and as the weeks go by, we forget that Jo is a right-brain, introverted, polka dotted, instigator and we just think Jo is an idiot.

How can Behavioural Economics help?

The core reason that team training fails to deliver sustainable performance is down to behavioural change. For effective behavioural change, you need to understand human decision-making and for that, there is Behavioural Economics.

Here is a taster of where Behavioural Economics can explain the breakdown of behavioural change.

We are more motivated to avoid loss than seek gain. The gain in this situation is that if everyone performs, we become a high performance unit. But that's not enough on a day-to-day basis to keep people behaving differently. Why? Because of what I have to lose.

Change means I have to give up what I'm used to (**Loss Aversion**), it requires more thinking and self-control than I can afford when I'm just trying to get my work done (depletion effect), and whilst the downside of having to spend time empathising with my colleague's style of thinking is blatantly obvious - I mean, who has the time?! - the payoff - "if this stuff even works" seems both ambiguous and way off on the horizon (**Short-term Bias**). And anyway, why should I if no one else is (**Social Norming**)?

To embed high performance you must design for it

To embed high performance, this is what you must do.

Design for the behavioural change.

First, use Behavioural Economics to understand what's inhibiting change, and on the flip side, what will motivate change. In the example above:
    * "Why should I when no one else is?" can instead become "I will because I see others doing it", and
    * "If this stuff even works" can instead become "I know what I need to do through small interactions to make a big difference overall"

And second, ensure that you have strategies to support both the motivation to change as well as ability to change.

In other words, the time to get your team to commit to new processes and policies, do the hard stuff like moving their office to be closer to their colleagues, and schedule meetings they don't like having is when they come back to the workplace highly motivated. Then, when motivation levels drop, the hard changes have already been taken care of so all that you require is the easier tasks. Morning teas, 'thank you' post-it notes...whatever you and your team have designated as 'easy' things should be rolled out so that even if no one really feels like it, you do it anyway and before you know it, you are on the path to high performance.

So by all means, learn from the best and aspire to create a high performance team; after all, the Sydney Swans did it. But you'll be wasting your money if you leave team performance at an intellectual level, assuming team members will change their behaviour on a rational basis.

To get your team to perform differently your task is one of behavioural change and for that, you need Behavioural Economics.

* The lowly football team has been updated from Port Adelaide to Essendon; proof that performance can change!

Based on an article originally published: 22 October 2012
http://briwilliams.com.au/articles/Blog--News-Why-team-training-falls-over-and-how-behavioural-economics-can-help

Four ways to motivate the unmotivated

Say you are a financial planner trying to convince a client to change their superannuation or a physio wanting to get your patient to do their exercises. Or imagine you are a manager who wants your staff to turn up on time, or a small business owner who want clients to pay on time.

How do you get the unmotivated to do what you want them to do?

It's probably the question I get asked the most often when I'm training health or finance professionals about habit and behaviour change. My seminar on the How of Habits, for instance, is about how to make changes once you have decided you want to.

But how can you get yourself or someone else to that point?

Here are four ways to approach it.

1. Make it so easy they do it without thinking

To get people to change behaviour we must first understand the relationship between motivation and ability.

Ability is our capacity and capability to do something and motivation is our desire to do so, and Stanford University Professor BJ Fogg's Behaviour Model outlines this beautifully(150).

Essentially, the harder something is to do, the greater the motivation required. The easier something is to do, the less motivation you need. That means if you make something easy to do you don't need to waste energy driving up motivation.

But how do you make things easy?

Make the behaviour you are trying to change really, really small. In fact BJ Fogg runs a Tiny Habits program based on this philosophy*(151)*. Instead of launching straight into running 5kms every day for example, which requires a lot of sustained motivation and willpower, the trick is to shrink the change down into steps that are so small they seem ridiculous. For example, putting sneakers on every morning for the first week.

I recently joined an online Cooking Habits program and for the first 5 days the only real behaviour I had to focus on was putting my chopping board out every night after I fed the dog*(152)*. No cooking. No recipes. Just putting the chopping board out. Why? Because once the board is out you can't help wanting to chop something!

By making things easy it is hard to wriggle out of a commitment to do it.

2. Design the environment

Making changes to the environment is a way to shape behaviour without having to think about it in the moment. I removed my office chair and got a standing desk so that I don't have to think about sitting down less - I have no choice.

But what happens if people have to be motivated to change their own environment?

Again, look for ways to make it easy. For instance ask them to:
   * store snacks on the top shelf in the pantry so they are harder to get to
   * hide their dessert spoons in a cupboard so they default to a sugar spoon when eating ice-cream
   * have their recharger in the laundry so they don't keep checking their phone
   * buy a small 'keep cup' so when buying coffee they default to the smaller size
   * only take cash to the shops rather than their credit card
   * arrange with their payroll office to divert a percentage of salary to a

savings account
    * keep their teabags or coffee in a low cupboard so every time they want
a cuppa they have to bend and stretch while the kettle boils

3. Get "Now Me" on board

Part of the issue with motivation is that it is required in the moment. In
order for me to act on superannuation, which benefits my "Future Me", I
need to enlist my "Now Me" present self to the cause to stop spending
money I should lock away.

The problem here is **Short-term Bias**, our desire for immediate
gratification, so to motivate someone who is not motivated we need to get
them to:
    * visualise themselves if they do make the change you are wanting them
to and
    * visualise themselves if they don't make the change

By probing them on how they will feel in the future you will bring those
feelings to the present and potentially spark enough motivation to get
them interested in change. Once you have that, talk with them about the
smallest change possible (refer point 1).

4. The Mary Poppins Principle

As Mary Poppins sang, "a spoon full of sugar makes the medicine go
down" and this is what's known as **Temptation Bundling**: combining
something we *should do* with something we *want to do.*

Your opportunity is to link the desirable behaviour with something they are
already doing such that they can only do the thing they love if they also do
the thing they lack motivation for. For example they can only watch their
favourite TV program at the gym.

Based on an article originally published: 13 July 2015
http://briwilliams.com.au/articles/Blog--News-4-ways-to-motivate-the-unmotivated

Why rational arguments fail (and what to do instead)

It's difficult to read a news article or watch someone being interviewed about their business decision-making without words like rational and logical being mentioned. Indeed "data driven decisions" is the war cry of this binary-crazed age.

It's a problem then, because we are fooling ourselves if we think that's how decisions are actually made.

Data-driven (as long as my gut agrees)

A report released by the Economist Intelligence Unit (EIU) called "Decisive Action: How businesses make decisions and how they could do better" surveyed 174 executives and senior managers from around the world about how they saw their style of decision-making and how they made decisions*(153)*.

According to the report 42% reported being "data driven",17% "empirical" and only 10% "intuitive". A further 32% described themselves as "collaborative".

So it is interesting that over two thirds (68%) of those who said they were "data driven" also said they trusted their own intuition when it came to decision-making. The number was even higher across all decision making types at 73%.

So what's going on here? I might describe myself as being data driven, but if that clashes with my gut instinct, then what?

According to the report, when asked "When taking a decision, if the available data contradicted your gut feeling, what would you do?" the most popular response (57% of respondents) was "Reanalyse the data" followed by "Collect more data" (30%). A mere 10% of these data-loving decision makers said they would "Take the course of action suggested by the data".

Huh?

Rational is in the eye of the beholder

This report shines a light on how mixed up we are when it comes to decision making. Data is proclaimed as king but often only used if it happens to coincide with gut instinct. If it doesn't, we keep looking.

And that's the challenge if you are trying to enlist support for your idea - you might pitch a business case or proposal that ticks all the 'rational' boxes and yet gets turned down.

The trick is to know that rational is in the eye of the beholder; a decision-maker will rationalise their reaction to data or analysis to accord with their own views held deep in their subconscious.

We've been pitching at the wrong level

In a sense, we've been focussing on the conscious, rational, logical centers of decision-making in business but ignoring the subconscious, intuitive, emotional drivers. And that's where the power lies.

Rational arguments fail because they are not engaging the real path to decision-making. To build a strong case you need to cover **why** you want to do something, **what** it is, **how** you'll do it, **who** will be involved, **when** you'll do it and **where** it will happen.

My guess is that you may be nailing these factors for the rational decision-making brain, particularly the what and why, but what about the 'non-rational'? What about things that will engage the sub-conscious?

How
How you communicate matters. For instance, you get to choose whether you describe the opportunity as one to save $10,000 or stop wasting $10,000. The same value from a rational perspective but the second has a much greater emotional kick due to **Loss Aversion**.

Who
What others are doing, matters. Your decision-maker will be persuaded by who you are and what other decision-makers might do.

When
The time horizon matters. People are driven by short-term needs and will be more persuaded by good stuff in the short term and leaving bad stuff till later. They will also make different decisions depending on the time of day you pitch.

Where
The environment in which the decision is made, matters. High or low ceilings, circular or angular seating, choice of typeface, noise levels and lighting can all impact decisions without the decision-maker being consciously aware.

Based on article originally published: 29 September 2014
http://briwilliams.com.au/articles/Blog--News-Why-rational-arguments-fail-and-what-you-should-do-instead

Chapter 13. Behavioural Strategies & Positioning

Pinpointing where your behavioural weaknesses lie

One of the trickiest parts of working out how to improve conversion is pinpointing the underlying behavioural cause.

So the first thing I do when I'm engaged to design a behavioural strategy for a client is a "back of the envelope" behavioural assessment of the product category in which they are competing for customer attention.

This framework is one you can use to get your head around why your online and offline conversion isn't where you want it to be.

Back of the Envelope Behavioural Assessment

This is my "back of the envelope" behavioural assessment, which I refer to as the "TICS Framework*(154)*".

$\mathcal{B}\mathcal{N}$'s Back of the Envelope Behavioural Assessment

T	Can they touch, see, taste, smell the reward for doing business with you? Tangible payoff ☐	*or*	☐	Intangible payoff
I	What's the timeframe for them to feel the payoff? Short term or long? Immediate benefit ☐	*or*	☐	Deferred benefit
C	How certain do they feel that they'll get what you're promising? Certain payoff ☐	*or*	☐	Uncertain payoff
S	Is this something that supports their positive self-perception? Congruent with self view ☐	*or*	☐	Incongruent with self view

The more ticks you get in the left hand column, the more the buyer will feel compelled to buy. Here you need to focus on minimising the Effort in doing business with you. The more in the right, the less compelled your buyer may feel. Focus on reducing anxiety and making the payoff (Rewards) more concrete.

There are 4 components to the TICS framework and I'm using product from two categories to highlight the differences: cars and life insurance.

T is for Tangibility
* Humans gravitate to things that are real. It's a greater leap of faith to buy a promise than it is a 'thing'. Just think how hard online retailers need to work to overcome customer Anxiety about sending payment into the ether compared with a shop front retailer who can hand over the goods there and then.
* Tangibility is an assessment of how tangible the payoff for buying the product or service is. Can they touch, taste, smell, see, hear the benefits? A new car is tangible, life insurance isn't. After all, you can't wrap your hands around "peace of mind".

I is for Immediacy
* Humans are motivated by instant gratification. We love getting good stuff now and leaving bad stuff till later. How soon does your customer feel the benefits of your product? For a new car, it's as soon as they get the keys. For life insurance, the payoff is (hopefully) way down the track - if not never!

C is for Certainty
* When it comes to buying something, customers like to know that the payoff will actually be delivered. Ambiguity evokes Anxiety so the clearer the outcomes the better. A new car is unequivocal whereas the life insurance category suffers from a (perhaps misguided) perception that policies won't be paid out.

S is for Self Perception
* How well does your product fit with the customer's self-perception? Humans seek an alignment between their values and behaviours, and will often adjust their values to remain congruent with something they have done. When it comes to buying something, customers need to ensure it fits with their internal narrative about the person they are. A new car is

likely to support a positive self-view (I deserve it because I work hard, it's for the safety of the kids etc.) whereas life insurance can jar with positive sense of self. In this case "I'm a good person for looking after my loved ones when I die" needs to overcome the tension of imagining yourself dead.

Let's use the framework to compare the behavioural challenges for a new car manufacturer vs. life insurance provider.

Car vs Life Insurance Behavioural Assessment

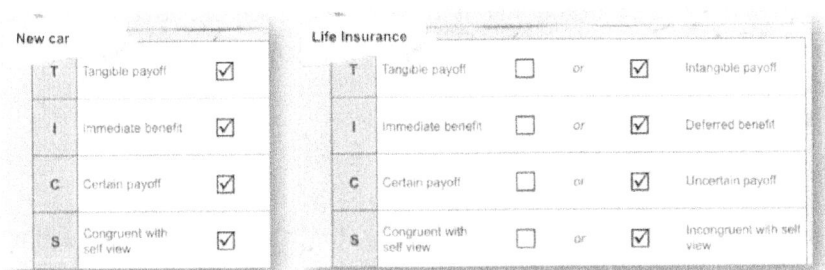

How do you stack up?

Once you've completed the assessment you will get a feel for where your main behavioural problems lie.

Happy days, I'm mainly in the left-hand column!

 * You most probably sell products rather than services, or the services you sell have obvious outcomes (like hairdressers and accountants rather than hypnotherapists or health retreats) and what you sell is likely well understood or familiar. There's good news and bad.

 * The good news is that you have a stronger behavioural proposition to work with. The bad news is that you are at great risk of undifferentiated competition (easier to sell = more attractive to sell by more people). The focus for you is on minimising the effort involved both in choosing you over others and in transacting with you. In terms of my Effort vs. Reward equation, concentrate first on Effort.

Oh no, I'm mainly in the right hand column!

* You might be one of the many professional service firms that finds themselves grappling with intangibility and uncertainty (how can I convince someone of the benefits of a health retreat? How can I prove that my marketing proposal will work better than someone else?).

* For businesses like these or with products like Life Insurance whose payoff is distant, ambiguous and perhaps regarded with ambivalence, the focus needs to be on strategies to compensate for this. As far as Effort vs. Reward goes, you need to dial up the Reward.

* While the big ticket payoff might be in the longer term, what can you do to make your customer benefit today? One superannuation fund, for example gives its customers discount on insurance policies, bringing a benefit into the immediate term.

What now?

This is where the magic happens. Sorry, that's not tangible enough is it? The next layer to turn this into an actionable behavioural strategy is to overlay two things;

* **Costs:** We've so far covered how the buyer may regard your product in terms of the payoff on offer. The other side of the equation is the cost. For example, life insurance not only suffers because benefits are intangible, but gets a double blow when the financial cost of taking out a policy is extremely tangible. Ouch!

* **Behavioural Enablers:** For every positive and negative identified through the assessment there is an underpinning behavioural principle that can be activated to resolve it. For example, to address a lack of certainty that triggers Loss Aversion a business can provide money back guarantees and assurances.

Based on an article originally published: 14 April 2014
http://briwilliams.com.au/articles/Blog--News-Pinpointing-where-your-behavioural-weaknesses-lie

Top 10 Behavioural INFLUENCES

There are something like 150 biases and heuristics that influence behaviour. That's a lot to navigate if you want to apply Behavioural Economics to everyday business issues, say writing an email, putting a pitch together or pacifying a disgruntled customer.

So here are my top 10. I've packaged them into a mnemonic called I.N.F.L.U.E.N.C.E.S. Use it as your checklist when embarking on an activity designed to get someone to do something.

I mmediacy (Short-term Bias): We act for now not later, e.g. snack now and promise to eat salad for the rest of the week. Ask yourself: what's the immediate payoff and have I deferred any downside?

N orms (Social Norms): We do what others do, e.g. preferring a bustling restaurant to one that's empty. Ask yourself: How can I signal that the desired behaviour is what other people also do?

F raming: Context changes meaning, e.g. black pearls became highly prized once they were associated with expensive gemstones. Ask yourself: What is my customer's frame of reference for this? With what am I compared?

L oss Aversion: We are more motivated to avoid loss than seek gain, e.g. second serve in tennis is more conservative than the first because there is something to lose. Ask yourself: What does my customer have to lose and how do I negate this?

U niqueness: We like our individuality to be recognised, not compromised, e.g. personalised Nutella and Coke. Ask yourself: Does my customer feel special and acknowledged?

E nvironment: Location and surroundings shape behaviour, e.g. bigger bowl leads to more ice-cream being consumed. Ask yourself: How can I shape the environment in which purchase and consumption take place?

N umbers: Contextualisation and display alter interpretation, e.g. 1,500.00 is perceived as larger than 1500. Ask yourself: Have I made painful numbers look small?

C hoice (Paradox of choice): We desire the freedom to choose but can be overwhelmed by it, e.g. 10x jams sold when fewer on display. Ask yourself: Have I reduced options to 3-5?

E ffort (vs. Reward): For behaviour to happen, Reward must be greater than Effort (R>E=B), e.g. Amazon 1-click. Ask yourself: Have I removed points of unnecessary effort?

S tatus Quo Bias: When in doubt we leave things as they are, e.g. leaving superannuation in the default fund. Ask yourself: What am I doing to budge people from their existing status quo? What do I want the new status quo to be?

P.S. You can download a PDF copy of I.N.F.L.U.E.N.C.E.S. from www.briwilliams.com.au/BE-for-business-resources

Based on an article originally published: 24 March 2016
http://www.briwilliams.com.au/articles/Blog--News-Top-10-behavioural-
INFLUENCES

Breaking macro behavioural challenges into micro ones

The 1880s were a time of change in Europe, with industrial and scientific breakthroughs set against a declining interest in Impressionism.

Steeled by the rejection of his latest painting by the Paris Salon, Georges Seurat turned to a community of likeminded artists in the Groupe des Artistes Independants, a collective seeking the advancement of modern art. And a new form of art was born.

After two years of work, in 1886 and aged 27, Seurat's acclaimed "*A Sunday Afternoon on the Island of La Grande Jatte*" heralded the creation of a new style of painting.

Pointillism, paintings comprised of hundreds of tiny colourful dots, fused art with the new scientific study of colour. Tricking the eye, Seurat's paintings from a distance look smooth and regular, but up close you see the individual spots of perfectly orchestrated paint.

And so it is with behaviour change. What we see from a distance belies the nuance underneath. Big changes are made up of smaller ones.

For instance, to change the conversion on a website, a macro challenge, we need to overcome micro-moments of anxiety about who you are, whether they are on the site they intended, how you can help them, where they should click first, what happens if they click and so on.

To sell more in your shop, consider things like whether customers feel they are getting 'sold to', whether their choices will be scrutinised by you, who else is watching, whether they can find the item cheaper elsewhere, and whether this item is what they actually want.

For customers looking to improve their health, it's about micro-moments when they are in the supermarket deciding what to put into their basket, whether to open the pantry when they are bored, choosing the escalator over the stairs, and feeling intimidated when they walk in the gym for a tour and more.

The good news is that the Behaviour Change Model can be applied to behavioural challenges both large and small.

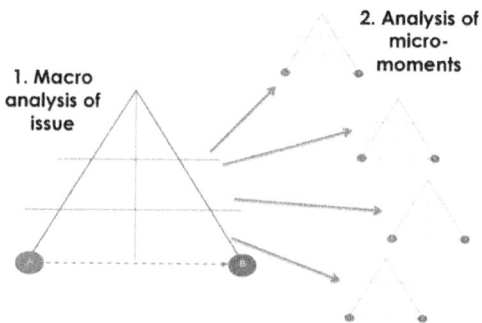

Delayering the behavioural challenge

Let's look at an example of how a macro issue can be delayered into smaller behavioural elements. Say we want to get younger people to contribute more to their compulsory superannuation – a macro issue.

Here's how we could analyse the macro behavioural barriers.

   * Apathy – more interesting things to think about right now, peers don't seem to be concerned, no idea of what future needs will be whereas present needs are clear

   * Paralysis – overwhelmed by the number of (conflicting) messages about investment strategy, overwhelmed by number of options presented by your firm

   * Anxiety – fear of locking away money that they may need, fear of returns not being guaranteed

This gives us a sense of where we need to strengthen our proposition to encourage action.

Now let's say we want people to click a button on a website, a micro-moment challenge, that just happens to be for superannuation.

   * **Apathy** - not clear why they should bother to click the button, more interested in visiting YouTube to watch the ad

   * **Paralysis** – overwhelmed by number of calls to action on the page

   * **Anxiety** – fear of clicking a button when they don't know where it leads, fear of clicking the wrong button

This gives us a sense of what we need to do to improve the odds of someone clicking the button – a clear Call to Action (CTA) where benefits of clicking outweigh and downside, and the CTA is the most enticing element on the page.

Design your behavioural change like a Seurat painting

You therefore have two levels of task when it comes to behaviour change; macro and micro. Only through the sum of parts, encouraging people to take all the small actions, will you be able to change behaviour on a larger scale. Concentrate on the dots and a beautiful picture will finally emerge.

Based on an article originally published: 10 November 2014
http://www.briwilliams.com.au/articles/Blog--News-Joining-the-dots-to-change-behaviour

Micro-moments matter

The two ads below are trying to do the same thing - get customers to buy more wine by promoting volume discounts, but that's where the similarity ends.

On the left Option A "Combined price" promotes the total price paid, so for one bottle $13, $22 for 2 and $27 for three.

On the right Option B "Averaged price" instead promotes the average for each bottle paid, so $12 each when you buy 2, $10 for 3 and $8 per bottle if you buy six.

Imagine this ad is your responsibility

Which way do you go? How do you know which will be more effective before you commit to printing the catalogue? Can you know? Is there any difference anyway?

This is what I mean by a micro-moment. In business you have to make decisions like this each and every day; decisions that seem small but can have a massive bearing on whether you succeed or fail.

While you might not be selling wine, you are most certainly selling something such as an idea, a business case or your services. You have a fraction of a second to convince your customer to do business with you and you better not stuff it up. One of these marketers has. Which one?

Which ad used behavioural techniques more effectively and why?

Option B "Averaged price" that promotes the average per bottle has more effectively used behavioural techniques.

Here's why:

* When people buy wine they are use to the cost per bottle. If I'm used to paying $12 a bottle then $8 is going to seem like a good deal. Option A "Combined price" on the other hand requires the customer to do some mental gymnastics to work back to the average to know whether $27 is good value or not. Whatever you do, *do not make your customer have to think hard about how great the deal is.*

* Option A sequences the prices in ascending order so even though the cost per bottle and savings become more advantageous, all the customer sees is that $27 is a lot more than $13.

* Option B in contrast sequences the price per bottle in descending order so that $8 seems cheap compared with $12.

Relativity and **Anchoring** are two of the behavioural principles underpinning these ads. In essence, the way in which you sequence and contextualise prices matters a great deal and can make or break a micro-moment.

Based on an article originally published: 2 December 2013
http://www.briwilliams.com.au/articles/Blog--News-Heres-why-micro-moments-matter

Why it's better to be wanted than needed

Is it better to be wanted or needed? For too long businesses have clung to the proposition that meeting a customer need is the way to success when in fact it is the power of desire that really matters.

"There's no margin in needs" is a statement I came across somewhere in my travels and I wish I could properly attribute it to the author because it gets to the heart of understanding customer behaviour.

Customer behaviour is flawed behaviour. By that I mean that your customer's decision to purchase is subject to myriad influences that happen below conscious awareness. How they are feeling, what music is playing in the background, what colour a Call to Action button is, how many and what kind of people are around - all these factors shape whether your customer will buy.

While at first blush this seems like you as a business have little control over how decisions are made, in truth it means all you have to do is understand the patterns of these influences and design to maximise your conversion. And that starts by thinking less about needs and more about wants.

Wants create two types of margin

"There's no margin in needs" runs counter to the prevailing mantra that you should make products that people need. To 'need' something is seen as a compulsion, an unequivocal and irrefutable justification. 'Want', meanwhile, is seen as a discretionary choice, something that appeals to momentary desire. Where we've gone wrong is to assume 'need' is the only avenue to 'must-have'. As Apple has most potently demonstrated, no one needed a tablet but they sure had to have one.

In contrast when I was working as a product manager for a large publisher we built our business around serving people's needs for contact information. That strategy worked for over 130 years, but then someone who served that need better displaced us. By focussing on the needs-state we had entirely neglected the want-state. If people had wanted to use us - if we had been satisfying an emotional desire - we would have been less exposed to cannibalisation.

By creating a want you create two types of margin, a value margin because you can charge more but perhaps more importantly, a behavioural margin that provides a buffer from substitution.

Wants are your source of differentiation

"There's no margin in needs" really spells out the challenge of differentiation. These days there are so many ways to get needs met, it is the emotional 'want' that will get you customers.

   * Everyone needs an accountant - why would I want to use you?

   * Everyone need petrol - why should I want to stop at your station?

   * Everyone needs to bank their money - why would I want to bank with you?

   * Everyone can read a blog - why do I want to read yours?

When people want something, it becomes a need

People are masters of self-justification. When we do something we can readily rationalise why. After all, we wouldn't smoke, binge on chocolate, drink too much or drive too fast if we prioritised our health, but we do and we have reasons why our behaviour is okay.

The same goes for purchase decisions. When your customer really wants something the justification will start to form in their mind and your role is to help them do this. Last in stock, great price, one of a kind, high quality, lifetime guarantee, good for your family... all prompts that will help your customer tell themselves a convincing story and will turn a want into a need.

How to design for wants

Want is an emotional state so to create willingness to purchase you need to evoke tension between having and not having your product or service.

Whether you do this in person, over the phone, in your marketing or on your website, these are the two prompts that will generate tension through contrast:
    1. What their life looks like with the product/service
    2. What their life looks like without it. In short, what pain does your customer feel by not buying from you?

Bringing these contrasting visions to life will form the basis of how you tap into the emotion of your customers and for your business to be the one from whom they want to buy. And hey, who doesn't want that?

Based on an article originally published: 28 April 2014
http://www.briwilliams.com.au/articles/Blog--News-Is-it-better-to-be-wanted-or-needed

Chapter 14. Innovation

Self-disruption: Risking going back to go forward

Kodak, AOL, Yellow Pages, Dell, Microsoft, Blackberry, Nokia, and Blockbuster make an uncomfortably long list of big, once successful businesses that failed or are failing to disrupt themselves and in so doing watching new entrants claim their markets. In fact it is easier to find case studies of capitulation than it is regeneration.

Blogger and PwC Director Richard Blundell wrote about the self-disruption of Netflix, from DVD to online streaming subscription services*(155)*.

Realising the market was moving away from DVDs, Netflix did two remarkable things. They:
   * switched customers to lower priced streaming subscriptions, taking a hit to revenue, and
   * bolstered their content so that the customers would receive a great experience, taking a hit to their cost base.

Blundell charts the transition, but the short story is that the pain they swallowed by reengineering their business is now paying off big time. Australian accounting software company MYOB is similarly transitioning from pure software to cloud services as its market shifts.

Why don't we all self-disrupt?

It is easy in hindsight to point to companies that have failed to adapt. Surely they must have known? Having worked for two large organisations whose business models were dying I can say yes, they must have known. We all knew.

But it wasn't a question of awareness, it was a question of behaviour.

Overcoming behavioural blockers

To be self-disruptors like Netflix we need to overcome the following behavioural biases in ourselves and our workplace culture.

Loss Aversion: fear of losing is stronger than desire to gain.
* For example, a business might choose to offset revenue declines as a result of customer attrition by increasing prices on out-dated product pans for those customers remaining. In Netflix's case this would have meant keeping customers on higher priced DVD subscriptions rather than moving them to lower priced plans with greater longer term potential.

Short-term Bias: preference to act for now rather than later
* Making decisions to dress the financial year results rather than address viability beyond that exemplify Short-term Bias. Often compounded by bonuses and rewards based on short-term results, short-term biases in decision making mean we risk never getting around to reengineering like we should.
* Beware 'Band-Aid' solutions that attempt to mask a haemorrhage and "Quick Wins" like price hikes that are superficial. Netflix could have raised its DVD subscription price and coasted on good top line performance right up till the time it found it had no customers left and no future.

Sunk Cost: it's hard to walk away from something in which we've invested time, money or effort.
* We get used to how things are and build processes, systems and habits around them. Stepping away from anything that is entrenched (including beliefs) is psychologically and financially difficult. Netflix had a portfolio of DVD titles that it had to walk away from, as well as a known customer engagement model and yet they overcame this in order to reengineer their business.

Time to disrupt yourself

So what kind of case study do you want your business to be: capitulation or regeneration?

If you are in a business that is stuck in status quo while your market is changing around you, if you are frustrated that your leaders or staff are not responding with the urgency and commitment to change you need then look to engage people like me who can bring an external perspective to your situation and chart a course forward. Disrupting your business is hard work, but closing your business is harder.

Based on an article originally published: 9 December 2013
http://briwilliams.com.au/articles/Blog--News-Self-Disruption-Risking-going-back-to-go-forward

How to get traction for new ideas in your business

I wonder if this seems familiar to you? A subscriber wrote asking me for ideas on the following:

> *"I am hoping to convince my company that they should incorporate behavioural insights into our product and advice offers. They have asked me to organise my thoughts and share with them my plan. I would like to create a compelling pitch that captures how 'applied behavioural science' can drive business results. My goal is to gain commitment to move forward with the introduction of a behavioural insights team into our organisation."*

This was exactly what I was faced with 6 years ago when I was still in the corporate sector. I knew about Behavioural Economics, and I could see the opportunity for our business so my task was trying to convince the unconvinced to change their behaviour.

I failed.

Long story short I ended up so frustrated by the reaction and so excited by the potential that I left and established my business, People Patterns.

To save you taking such dramatic action I can tell you how I now go about convincing the unconvinced, and would have had I known what I do now.

Preparation

As with all behavioural challenges, start by articulating the current and desired stakeholder behaviours. This will help you focus on what the change task actually amounts to. In other words, what are they currently doing, and what do you want them to do?

Then it's a matter of anticipating the behavioural reasons for resistance by analysing each of the three reasons for inertia, and identifying ways to overcome these barriers.

   * **Apathy/laziness** (System 1) – what are the ingrained organisational habits around customer insights and why should they bother expending effort getting across yet another field?

   * **Paralysis** (Paradox of Choice) – is there any risk of overwhelming them? How many options will you present and in what sequence?

   * **Anxiety** (Loss Aversion) - why might they feel anxious about adopting behavioural insights? Why should they feel anxious about not adopting Behavioural Economics?

Presentation

Once you've done your preparation, your attention should turn to crafting a compelling presentation that has three elements.

1. Tension

All effective websites, TV ads, sitcoms, books, movies and yes, presentations have tension built in to their narrative. Why? Because to shake the habitual System 1 Elephant out of its stupor and get it engaged we need to do something that is salient, surprising and/or scary.

Salient – Why is this important? Contextualise the presentation in terms of what's important to the business but not being taken care of. I often use the "where BE fits" model (Chapter 1) to show how Behavioural Economics fits a gap that no other form of insights currently does.

Surprising– What can you tell them they don't already know? How can you usurp their assumptions? For instance in my presentations I start by talking about the flawed assumptions we've made about how people behave, and why this means we've been doing business (or changing habits) in the wrong way.

Scary – What are the ramifications of not doing what you are suggesting? By drawing attention to the gap between what is known by the business and what needs to be known in order to win in market, you will make your audience feel anxious. Perhaps the quickest way to make them sweat is to point out who in their market has already adopted Behavioural Economics. Fear of being left behind is pretty compelling and once they feel uneasy they will be motivated to seek answers. At that point they will be raring to get your solution.

2. What's In It For Me? (WIIFM)

Everyone in your audience is thinking about themselves – how will this help me? How will this hurt me? While their questions might be phrased in corporate speak ("I'm just not convinced it aligns with our BAU or strategic priorities. We're looking to leverage synergies between our blah blah blah…"), all they are really telling you is I DON'T GET WHAT'S IN IT FOR ME?

The worst approach is to bang on about yourself. "I'm from (Boring Co)… I'm here to (talk about myself) today…". Businesses do it on their websites and people do it in their pitches thinking it establishes credibility. NO. It bores people. It switches them off. It needs to be about them – what you've noticed about their situation, some home truths (which builds intrigue because you are pointing to a gap), and through that process you gain credibility. Always ask and answer "Why is this important for them to know?"

3. Structure
I've alluded to it already, but crafting your presentation is like a 3 Act play. It needs a beginning, middle and end;
   * **Beginning** – the gap, why this presentation is important for them
   * **Middle** – the guts of what it means, how your solution looks
   * **End** – the resolution, all it takes from here

There's a lot more I could say about why Behavioural Economics is so important for businesses to get their heads around - for instance I could point to how it's being used by Google, Barclays, The Red Cross, the US, UK, NSW and Victorian governments, Australia's leading banks and superannuation providers, numerous ad agencies and utilities providers (and all of my clients, obviously) and I could point to it being the field of science that gives you results without costing you anything more, but for now I'll leave you with an approach that I wish I had had all those years ago to convince the unconvinced.

Based on an article originally published: 5 October 2015

http://briwilliams.com.au/articles/Blog--News-How-to-get-traction-in-your-business

Chapter 15. Final thoughts

It was around 2009 when my brother gave me a book that changed my life: "Predictably Irrational" by Dan Ariely. Not only did the unconscious influences on customer behaviour start to make sense but at last I saw a way to fuse my qualifications in finance and psychology: Behavioural Economics.

It lead me to start a blog on the subject, which in turn lead to a regular column for Smartcompany and me writing my first book, "*22 Minutes to a Better Business*". Such was my passion for the emerging field that in 2011 I left the security of a corporate role to start my business, People Patterns, the first consultancy in Australia to specialise in the application of Behavioural Economics to everyday business issues.

So I know from personal experience the power a book can have.

While that book and many like it since have made the world of behavioural science accessible to those in business, they have stopped tantalisingly short of explaining how to influence customers at the coalface.

I hope this book has bridged that gap. It was my aim to provide you a workable, scalable and easy to apply framework so you can use Behavioural Economics with confidence. I wanted to engage you, clarify your choices and overcome any anxiety you have about applying these techniques to your business.

We've covered a lot of ground.

Part I. Business is about changing behaviour, which included:
  * The role of Behavoural Economics
  * Williams Behaviour Change Model
  * How to identify and address Apathy
  * How to identify and address Paralysis
  * How to identify and address Anxiety

Williams Behaviour Change Model

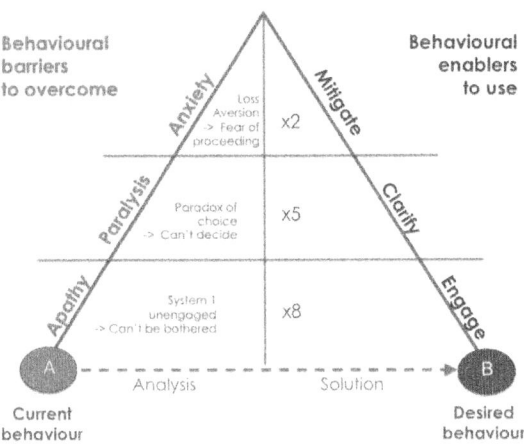

Part II: Applied Behavioural Economics, which included:
  * Behavioural Economics by Business Type
  * Market Research and Customer Insights
  * Pricing
  * Acquisition
  * Retention
  * Website Design
  * People Management
  * Behavioural Strategies and Positioning
  * Innovation

In the following pages you'll find the third and final section of this book.

Part III: Resources and References, which includes:
  * Williams Behaviour Change Model and Worksheet
  * Access to an exclusive online resource centre
  * Glossary of acronyms used in this book
  * Glossary of behavioural biases, heuristics and principles
  * An index of organisations mentioned mentioned in this book
  * Footnote references

With that I would like to thank you for your interest in Behavioural Economics, and how it may be applied to improve business outcomes.

Good luck, and keep behaving.

Part III.

Resources and References

Williams Behavioural Change Model Diagram

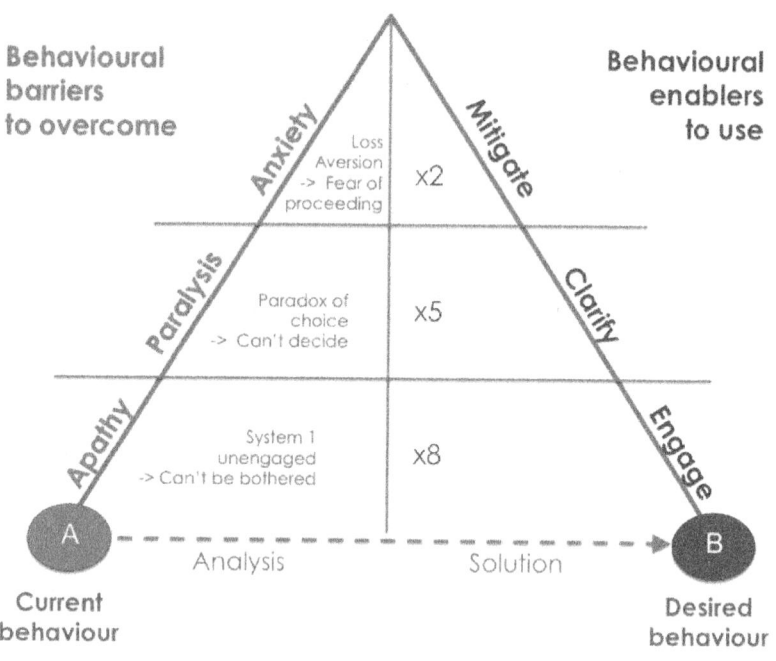

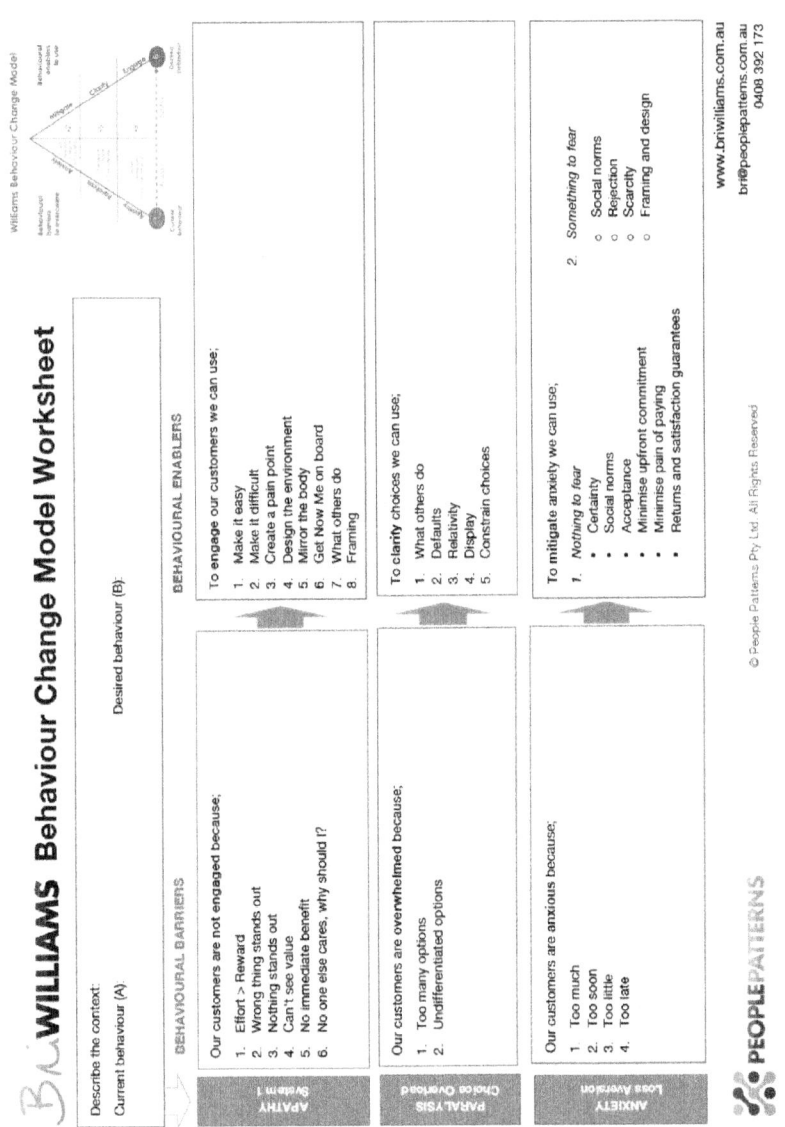

BRi WILLIAMS Behaviour Change Model Worksheet

Describe the context:

Current behaviour (A):   Desired behaviour (B):

BEHAVIOURAL BARRIERS

Our customers are not engaged because;

1. Effort > Reward
2. Wrong thing stands out
3. Nothing stands out
4. Can't see value
5. No immediate benefit
6. No one else cares, why should I?

APATHY
System 1

Our customers are overwhelmed because;

1. Too many options
2. Undifferentiated options

PARALYSIS
Choice Overload

Our customers are anxious because;

1. Too much
2. Too soon
3. Too little
4. Too late

ANXIETY
Loss Aversion

BEHAVIOURAL ENABLERS

To **engage** our customers we can use;

1. Make it easy
2. Make it difficult
3. Create a pain point
4. Design the environment
5. Mirror the body
6. Get Now Me on board
7. What others do
8. Framing

To **clarify** choices we can use;

1. What others do
2. Defaults
3. Relativity
4. Display
5. Constrain choices

To **mitigate** anxiety we can use,

1. *Nothing to fear*
   - Certainty
   - Social norms
   - Acceptance
   - Minimise upfront commitment
   - Minimise pain of paying
   - Returns and satisfaction guarantees

2. *Something to fear*
   o Social norms
   o Rejection
   o Scarcity
   o Framing and design

Williams Behaviour Change Model

www.briwilliams.com.au
bri@peoplepatterns.com.au
0408 392 173

PEOPLEPATTERNS

Download a softcopy of this worksheet at
www.briwilliams.com.au/BE-for-business-resources

Behavioural Economics for Business
Online Resource Centre

Additional resources are available for you at:
www.briwilliams.com.au/BE-for-business-resources

The resources include;
* Behaviour Change Worksheet
* Top 10 Behavioural INFLUENCES PDF
* TICS framework
* Customer retention diagram
* Some of my favourite research studies

And much more.

Glossary of Acronyms

ATL	Above the Line (advertising)
B2B	Business-to-Business
B2C	Business-to-Consumer
BE	Behavioural Economics
BI	Behavioural Insights
CEO	Chief Executive Officer
C-Suite	Refers to "Chief" roles within an organisation e.g. Chief Executive Officer (CEO), Chief Information Officer (CIO), Chief Financial Officer (CFO)
CTA	Call to Action
FOMO	Fear Of Missing Out
PIN	Personal Identification Number
PR	Public Relations
PWYW	Pay What You Want pricing
RRP	Recommended Retail Price
ROI	Return on Investment
TICS	Tangibility, Immediacy, Certainty, Self-worth
WIIFM	What's In It For Me?

Glossary of Behavioural Biases, Heuristics and Principles

Listed below are key behavioural biases, heuristics and principles. Those covered in this book are in **bold**.

Actor-Observer Bias (Fundamental Attribution Error): Tendency to attribute own behaviour to character and the behaviour of others to the situation.

Adaption: Tendency for the impact to wear off the more something is experienced.

Affect Heuristic: What we like determines our beliefs.

Ambiguity: We tend to avoid options where incomplete information makes the choice feel risky.

Anchoring: We base decisions on information that has been previously introduced even if it's irrelevant.

Attentional Bias: We tend to focus on only one or two choices even when there are several possible outcomes.

Authority: Tendency to defer to someone who seems to be in authority.

Availability Bias: Information that easily comes to mind tends to be over-weighted in its importance.

Availability Cascade: A simple idea gains popularity because of how simple it is, then seems even more simple because of how popular it is.

Backfire Bias: We reject evidence that contradicts our point of view even if we know it's true.

Behavioural Economics: The study of social, cognitive and emotional biases and heuristics that influence economic decision-making behaviour.

Bias Blind spots: We fail to see our own cognitive biases.

Biases: Hard-wired decision-making tendencies. See also Heuristics.

Bounded Rationality: our rationality has limits.

Centre Stage Effect (a.k.a Goldilocks Effect): Tendency to prefer the middle option.

Certainty (Zero risk) Bias: We are influenced more by smaller changes in probability that provide certainty than larger changes that do not. ie 99% to 100% better than 50% to 60%

Choice Architecture: Structuring choices so optimal decisions can be made.

Choice Bracketing: Tendency to focus on the impact of individual choices rather than the consequences of many choices taken together.

Choice Overload: More choices can result in less choosing. See also Paradox of Choice.

Choice Supportive Bias: We think positively about the choice once made even if it has flaws.

Clustering illusion: We tend to identify patterns where none are present.

Cognitive Dissonance: The tension we feel when our actions and beliefs are not consistent.

Commitment Devices: Tools to lock us in to our intended behaviour.

Completion Bias (a.k.a. Endowed Progress): We are driven to complete tasks once we have started.

Confirmation Bias: We tend to seek information that confirms rather than contradicts our view.

Conjunction fallacy: We tend to believe the probability of two events happening is greater than one.

Consistency Bias: Incorrectly remembering one's past attitudes and behaviour as resembling present attitudes and behaviour.

Conservatism Bias: Reliance on prior evidence rather than new information, e.g. the world is flat.

Contra Free Loading: Tendency to pay for things we value and work for reasons other than money.

Curse of Knowledge: The more informed of us don't get why others cannot understand.

Decoupling: Tendency to separate the cost from the benefit over time.

Decision Quicksand: The tendency to seek additional information when an easy decision becomes unexpectedly difficult.

Decoy Effect: We can be persuaded to change our preferences between two choices when a third option is presented.

Default Bias (a.k.a. Status Quo Bias): Tendency to want things to stay the same, selecting the default option where available.

Denominator Neglect: We focus on the number of times something has happened rather than the overall number of opportunities for it to happen.

Depletion Effect: The more decisions made in a day the more our capacity to make new ones is reduced. See also Ego Depletion.

Diagnosis Bias: We jump to an initial assessment from which it is difficult to change.

Disfluency: When information is difficult to process it interrupts processing fluency and increases perceived effort. See also Processing Fluency.

Disposition Effect: Tendency to sell shares whose price has increased, while keeping assets that have dropped in value to avoid being reminded of 'failure'.

Distinction Bias: We value two options differently when looking at them together rather than separately.

Diversification Bias: We overestimate the amount of variety we'll actually need in the future.

Drop in the Bucket Effect: Tendency to not act if the impact of a personal contribution is not easily discerned.

Dual Process Theory: Conceptualisation of how we process information using two systems; e.g. conscious and unconscious, System 1 and System 2.

Duration Neglect: When the duration doesn't factor into the valuation.

Effort vs. Reward: Conceptualisation of the two elements of behavioural influence; resources expended compared with the payoff. For behaviour to happen, R must exceed E.

Ego Depletion: Tendency to make easy (default or impulsive) decisions once System 2 has been exhausted. See also Depletion Effect

Empathy Gap: Our inability to understand people in a different emotional state to us.

Endowed Progress (a.k.a. Completion Bias): We are driven to complete tasks once we have started.

Endowment Effect (Ikea Effect): Value things we own more than things we don't and demand much more to give it up than others are willing to pay.

Focussing illusion: Whatever we are thinking about at that moment seems more important than at any other time.

Framing: Tendency to draw different conclusions depending on how the data is presented.

Free: We act with disproportionate force when something is free. It can persuade us to change our behaviour.

Frequency illusion: Something you've just learned appears to be everywhere.

Goldilocks Effect (a.k.a.Centre Stage Effect): Tendency to prefer the middle option.

Halo Effect: We carry judgments about one characteristic over to another.

Hard-Easy Bias: We tend to be over confident on easy problems and not confident enough for those that are hard.

Hedonic Framing: Two separate gains are more valuable than one large gain of equal value, whereas two separate losses are more painful than a single loss of equal value.

Herding (Bandwagon Effect): Tendency to base actions and beliefs on what others are doing or believing. See also Social Norms.

Heuristics (Rules of Thumb): Governing cultural, social or personal 'rules' we live our lives by. These mental short-cuts save mental energy but may be sub optimal. E.g. Price=quality; house brands are cheaper.

Hindsight Bias: We trick ourselves into believing we "knew it all along" rather than admit error.

Hyperbolic Discounting: 'Bird in the hand'. We tend to value a gain we receive now more than a larger gain available in the future. See also Short-term Bias.

Ideometer Effect: When an idea causes an unconscious physical reaction.

Illusion of control: We overestimate our ability to control events.Illusion of validity: We tend to believe our predictions are valid despite contradictory evidence, e.g. product breakdowns

Impact Bias (Affective Forecasting Error): We overestimate how happy or sad we will feel in the future about a gains or loss.

Information Avoidance: "Head in the sand" avoidance of information that would result in a negative outcome.

Inter Group Bias: We view people in our own group differently than someone in another group.

Inter-temporal Choice (a.k.a. Short-term Bias): We tend to focus on the immediate result of a decision over what the future may be.

Irrational Escalation: Investing more in something based on the past even if we know its bad, throwing 'good money after bad'.

Judgment Heuristic: The methods we use to simplify our decision making and assessments of probability.

Just World Hypothesis: Our desire to believe that a higher power, karma, forces of justice or stability guide situations.

Less is More: Perversely, with less knowledge we can often make more accurate predictions.

Loss Aversion: We prefer to avoid losses because they are 1.5-2.5 times as painful as gains are pleasurable.

Mary Poppins Principle: My description of Temptation Bundling, where you improve the likelihood of action by bundling a "want to do" with a "should do" (i.e. spoon full of sugar helps the medicine go down).

Mental accounting: Tendency to think of the world in terms of specific accounts where value in one account is different to other.

Mood Heuristic: Our mood affects ratings and judgments.

Narrative Fallacy: The way we have constructed our story of the past leads to imperfect decisions in the future.

Negativity Bias: We place more emphasis on negative experiences than positive.

Not Invented Here Bias: Tendency to dismiss the ideas of others.

Observer-Expectancy Effect: Our expectations influence how we perceive an outcome.

Omission Bias: We tend to judge harmful actions as worse than equally harmful inactions.

Outcome Bias: We judge a decision on the outcome rather than the quality of the decision, ignoring the role luck plays.

Over Optimism: Tendency to think the world is better than it is, leaving us unprepared for danger and vulnerable to violence.

Over Confidence: We are too confident in our abilities which causes risk taking in every day lives.

Paradox of Choice: We like the freedom to choose but can get overwhelmed by it. See also Choice Overload.

Pessimism: Tendency to overweigh negative consequences.

Placebo Effect: Self-fulfilling prophecy where our beliefs cause something to happen.

Planning Fallacy: tendency to underestimate the length of time something will take, overestimate benefits and underestimate costs.

Possibility Effect: tendency to overweight the importance of highly unlikely events.

Pre Decisional Distortion: Tendency to 'imprint' on brand initially favoured due to specific attribute and then sequentially judge other brands relative to that lead brand, e.g. home security

Priming: Our acts are often influenced by sub-conscious cues.

Procedural Fairness: We tend to accept an outcome if we believe the process has been fair.

Processing Fluency: The ease with which information is understood can impact behaviour. See also Disfluency.

Prospect Theory: We make judgments relative to reference points and losses are more influential than gains.

Recency: We weight latest information more heavily than older information.

Reciprocity: Fairness should trump other values even if it's not in the interests of the economy or other parties.

Regression to the Mean: Tendency for aggregate behaviour to be drawn close to the average and to take credit for rebalancing.

Relativity: Everything is judged relative to something else and we prefer to use obvious rather than difficult points of comparison.

Remembering vs. Experiencing Self: We are persuaded by not only the experience but our memory of it.

Representativeness (Belief Bias): We assume things with some similarities are more similar than they really are.

Restraint Bias: We overestimate our ability to show restraint in the face of temptation.

Revenge: We will act to punish another due to perceived wrongdoing.

Salience: We focus on easily recognisable or memorable features of a person or concept.

Satisficing: Settling for 'good enough' rather than optimal decisions

Scarcity: Tendency to value something more if it is rare.

Seer Sucker Illusion: We rely too heavily on expert advice, avoiding responsibility.

Selective Perception: We allow our expectations to influence how we perceive the world.

Self-Enhancing Transmission Bias: We share our successes more than our failures, creating a false perception of reality and an inability to accurately assess situations.

Self-Herding: Tendency to follow decisions we have taken before.

Short-term Bias (a.k.a. Present Bias, Inter-Temporal Bias): Preference for immediate gratification and to defer bad news till later. See also Hyperbolic Discounting.

Size Congruency Effect: Larger font is processed to mean bigger price and vice versa.

Small Area Hypothesis: We are more motivated to complete our goal if our attention is directed to the smaller representation of progress (e.g. "Only 10% to go" rather than "You are 90% through")

Social Norms: Tendency to follow what others do, the 'normal; behaviour in a situation. See also Herding.

Status Quo Bias (a.k.a. Default Bias): Tendency to want things to stay the same, selecting the default option where available.

Stereotyping: We expect a group of people to have certain qualities without having any real information about the individuals.

Sunk Cost Fallacy: Tendency to maintain possession of a position or item because of the resources already put in rather than give it up.

Survivorship Bias: We focus on examples of things that have survived (e.g. business success rather than failure rates).

System 1: Fast, intuitive, automatic, habitual, instinctive thinking. Vast capacity 11,000,000 bits/second (i.e. Elephant.)

System 2: Slow, rational, logic and fact driven thinking. Limited capacity 40-50 bits/second (i.e. Rider.)

Temptation Bundling (a.k.a. Mary Poppins Principle)**:** Improving the likelihood of action by bundling a "want to do" with a 'should do".

Tragedy of Commons: We overuse common resources because it is not in our individual interest to conserve them.

Transaction Utility: We are predisposed to pay more for something that we visualise in an expensive setting.

Uniqueness: We prefer to think we are unique, and will react against forces that compromise our sense of individuality.

Unit Bias: The belief that there is a universally agreed optimal unit size.

Up/Down congruence: Matching value representations to the head (up) and heart (down).

Visual Depiction Effect: Tendency to be persuaded by images oriented for use.

Vividness: tendency to respond to something that stands-out.

An up-to-date glossary of biases, heuristics and principles is maintained at: www.briwilliams.com.au/behavioural-economics-glossary

Index of Organisations

An alphabetical list of organisations mentioned in this book.

Footnote References

1. Packaging: Vivian Zurlo and Candace Dunn shared this case study at the Mumbrella Retail Marketing Summit, February 2016

2. Polling: http://www.nytimes.com/2015/06/21/opinion/sunday/whats-the-matter-with-polling.html?smprod=nytcore-iphone&smid=nytcore-iphone-share&_r=1

3. Eating habits: http://mobile.abc.net.au/news/2015-06-22/unhealthy-eating-habits-the-new-normal-for-victorians-study/6562924

4. Craft beer: http://qz.com/420295/americans-claim-to-love-craft-beer-but-they-actually-buy-bud-light/

5. GLAD: http://www.smartcompany.com.au//marketing/45309-glad-australia-cops-backlash-over-clingwrap-changes-80-metres-of-sheer-frustration/

6. Parole judgments: Danziger, S., Levav, J., Avnaim-Pesso, L. *"Extraneous factors in judicial decisions"*. Proceedings of the National Academy of Sciences, 2011

7. Processing fluency: Song, H., and Schwartz, N. *"If It's Hard to Read, It's Hard to Do: Processing Fluency Affects Effort Prediction and Motivation"* 2008 https://dornsife.usc.edu/assets/sites/780/docs/08_ps_song___schwarz_effort.pdf

8. Exercise instructions: Of course this is the type of experiment that could benefit from another layer of testing – one in which participant exercise behaviour was observed rather than self-reported.

9. Ice-cream bowls: Wansick, B., Van Ittersum, K., and Painter J. *"Ice cream illusions bowls, spoons, and self-served portion sizes"*. Am J Prev Med. 2006 Sep; 31(3):240-3.

10. Ice-cream study: The participants were nutritionists, proving that just because you know what you should do, doesn't mean you necessarily will.

11. In store music: North, A., Hargreaves, D. McKendrick, J. *"The influence of in-store music on wine selections"*. Journal of Applied Psychology, Vol 84(2), Apr 1999, 271-276.

12. Seating arrangements: Zhu, R. and Argo, J. "Exploring the Impact of Various Shaped Seating Arrangements on Persuasion." *Journal of Consumer Research*: August 2013.

13. Where we sit: "Slim by Design: Mindless eating solutions for everyday life" by Brian Wansink http://www.slimbydesign.org

14. Spock vs. Captain Kirk: attributed to Richard Thaler

15. Target's data: http://www.nytimes.com/2012/02/19/magazine/shopping-habits.html?pagewanted=1&_r=2&hp

16. B.E. Definition: I'm a pragmatist rather than purest, by the way, so while some may take issue with my lay explanation of Behavioural Economics, my role is to move beyond terminology and get to the heart of what it means for you in your business.

17. History: Richard Thaler's *"Misbehaving"* offers a history of Behavioural Economics

18. Gap in literature: As good a job as these books are doing in bringing behavioural research to the business public, they are still written from the perspective of the research rather than its application to business. I started to address this deficit in 2011 with my book *"22 Minutes to a Better Business"*, and more extensively in the book you are now reading.

19. Rebranding psychology: Even if it is simply rebranding psychology as "Behavioural Economics", what a great demonstration of the principle of "framing", proving that how something is communicated can be as important as what is communicated.

20. Procter's trial: http://www.mycustomer.com/service/contact-centres/behavioural-economics-in-the-call-centre-to-be-or-not-to-be?utm_source=feedburner&utm_medium=feed&utm_campaign=FeedA%20mycustomer/all%20%28MyCustomer.com%29%4

21. Westpac's app (video): https://www.youtube.com/watch?v=M9v9HpR4qTU

22. Ikea's architecture: http://thehappycity.com/how-ikea-uses-architecture-to-trick-you-into-buying-stuff/

23. Domino's campaigns: http://www.marketingmagazine.co.uk/article/1068007/dominos-integrate-behavioural-economics

24. Birmingham Airport: https://www.research-live.com/article/features/ready-for-takeoff/id/4007319

25. Hi there: This is a special spare footnote to say I hope you are enjoying the book.

26. US Cellular via Tibco (video): http://media.tibco.com/loyalty-lab/adobe-presenter/uscc/

27. Amp app: http://ampformarketing.com/amp-ipad-app-press-release

28. Results: Elizabeth Ball, It's In The Stars

29. M.I.N.D.S.P.A.C.E.: The first framework designed by the UK Behavioural Insights team, MINDSPACE pulls together nine "robust influences on human behaviour and change", and is an excellent capture of the major principles.

* **M** essenger – we are heavily influenced by who communicates

information

* **I** ncentives – our responses to incentives are shaped by predictable mental shortcuts, such as strongly avoiding losses

* **N** orms – we are strongly influenced by what others do

* **D** efaults – we 'go with the flow' of pre-set options

* **S** alience – our attention is drawn to what is novel and seems relevant to us

* **P** riming – our acts are often influenced by sub-conscious cues

* **A** ffect – our emotional associations can powerfully shape our actions

* **C** ommitment – we seek to be consistent with our public promises, and reciprocate acts

* **E** go – we act in ways that make us feel better about ourselves

More: www.behaviouralinsights.co.uk/publications/mindspace/

30. E.A.S.T.: Also devised by the UK government's Behavioural Insights Team, the EAST framework endeavours to further simplify a behavioural framework to "make more effective and efficient policy".

* **E** asy – simplifying the message, reducing points of friction and using defaults

* **A** ttractive – attracting attention and using rewards and incentives to stimulate action

* **S** ocial – normalising the desired behaviour and encouraging people to make commitments

* **T** imely – getting people at the right time with a proposition that is weighted in favour of short-term benefits

More: http://www.behaviouralinsights.co.uk/publications/east-four-simple-ways-to-apply-behavioural-insights/

31. I.N.F.L.U.E.N.C.E.S.: My top 10 list of behavioural principles which includes;

* **I** mmediacy (Short-term Bias): We act for now not later. e.g. snack now and promise to eat salad for the rest of the week.

 * **N** orms (Social Norms): We do what others do. e.g. preferring a bustling restaurant to one that's empty.

 * **F** raming: Context changes meaning. e.g. black pearls became highly prized once they were associated with expensive gemstones.

 * **L** oss Aversion: We are more motivated to avoid loss than seek gain. e.g. second serve in tennis is more conservative than the first because there is something to lose.

 * **U** niqueness: We like our individuality to be recognised, not

compromised. e.g. personalised Nutella and Coke.

  * **E** nvironment: Location and surroundings shape behaviour. e.g. bigger bowl leads to more ice-cream being consumed.

  * **N** umbers: Contextualisation and display alter interpretation. e.g. 1,500.00 is perceived as larger than 1500.

  * **C** hoice (Paradox of choice): We desire the freedom to choose but can be overwhelmed by it. e.g. 10x jams sold when fewer on display.

  * **E** ffort (vs. Reward): For behaviour to happen, Reward must be greater than Effort (R>E=B). e.g. Amazon 1-click.

  * **S** tatus Quo Bias: When in doubt we leave things as they are. e.g. leaving superannuation in the default fund.

More information in Chapter 14 and in the online resources.

32. Anti-smoking campaigns: Mahoney, J. *"Strategic communication and anti-smoking campaigns"* http://epress.lib.uts.edu.au/journals/index.php/pcr/article/viewFile/1868/1915

33. Stock choices: Kempf, A. and Ruenzi, S.*"Status Quo Bias and the Number of Alternatives: An Empirical Illustration from the Mutual Fund Industry"* Journal of Behavioral Finance, Vol. 7, No. 4, pp. 204-213, 2006.

34. Two heads: Daniel Kahneman's *"Thinking Fast and Slow"* describes System 1 (fast) and System 2 (slow) in detail

35. Data per second: Phil Barden, *"Decoded: The science behind why we buy"*

36. Elephant and the Rider: this metaphor was brought to life by Jonathan Haidt in *"The Happiness Hypothesis"*, and later popularised by authors Dan and Chip Heath in their book *"Switch"*.

37. Now Me and Future Me: Kelly McGonigal refers to You and You 2.0 in her book *"The Willpower Instinct"*. I can't recall who or where Now Me and Future Me came across my radar, but thanks to the person who used these descriptions

38. Virtuous Future Me: Read, D., Loewenstein, G. and Kalyanaraman, S. *"Mixing virtue and vice: combining the immediacy effect and the diversification heuristic"* 1999 Journal of Behavioral Decision Making Volume 12, Issue 4, pages 257–273

39. Food selection: http://foodpsychology.cornell.edu/outreach/preordering.html

40. Diversification Bias: Salisbury, L. and Feinberg, F. *"Future Preference Uncertainty and Diversification: The Role of Temporal Stochastic Inflation"* 2008 Journal of Consumer Research, Vol. 35

41. Insurance Ad: https://www.youtube.com/watch?v=UPwxNp0V4GA

42. Red Tomato: https://www.youtube.com/watch?v=-Y51eqhlnRY

43. Cutlery: https://chrisnorfield.wordpress.com/2014/08/07/a-simple-nudge-to-stop-staff-stealing-cutlery/

44. Car keys: http://www.pleasurabletroublemakers.com/keymoment-1/

45. Disfluency: From Adam Alter's presentation to The Wheeler Centre referenced http://www.briwilliams.com.au/articles/Blog--News-When-making-it-hard-for-customers-can-be-a-good-thing?mc_cid=7f0fa08cbe&mc_eid=[UNIQID]. For more read Alter's book *"Drunk Tank Pink"*.

46. Egg Theory: https://www.psychologytoday.com/blog/inside-the-box/201401/creativity-lesson-betty-crocker

47. StickK: https://www.stickk.com/faq

48. Temptation Bundling: http://freakonomics.com/podcast/when-willpower-isnt-enough-a-new-freakonomics-radio-podcast/

49. Eyedrops: http://www.briwilliams.com.au/articles/Blog--News-The-point-of-pain-to-influence-behaviour

50. Ceiling height: Meyers-Levy, J. and Zhu, R. *"Ceiling Height Can Affect How A Person Thinks, Feels And Acts."* ScienceDaily. ScienceDaily, 25 April 2007.

51. Voting: Berger, J., Meredith, M. and Wheeler, S. *"Contextual priming: Where people vote affects how they vote"* PNAS, July 1, 2008 vol. 105 no. 26

52. Seating: Zhu, R. and Argo, J. *"Exploring the Impact of Various Shaped Seating Arrangements on Persuasion."* 2013 Journal of Consumer Research

53. Shape of glass: Attwood A., Scott-Samuel N., Stothart G. and Munafò M. *"Glass Shape Influences Consumption Rate for Alcoholic Beverages"*. 2012 PLoS ONE 7(8)

54. Stale popcorn: Wansink, B. and Kim J. *"Bad popcorn in big buckets: portion size can influence intake as much as taste"*. 2005 J Nutr Educ Behav.37(5):242-5.

55. Red Pringle: Geier, A., Wansink, B. and Rozin, P. *"Red potato chips: Segmentation Cues and Consumption Interrupts Frame Portion Sizes and Reduce Food Intake"*. 2012 Health Psychology, 31, 398-401.

56. Ice-cream storage: Wansink, B., Just, D. and McKendry, J. 2010 http://www.nytimes.com/interactive/2010/10/21/opinion/20101021_Oplunch.html?_r=0)

57. Ibid

58. Centre-Stage Effect: Rodway, P., Schepman, A. and Lambert, J. *"Preferring the One in the Middle: Further Evidence for the Centre-stage Effect"* 2012 Applied Cognitive Psychology Volume 26, Issue 2, pages 215–222

59. Retail examples: Taken from http://briwilliams.com.au/articles/Blog--News-Shaping-the-environment-to-influence-your-customer

60. Google cafeteria: http://www.fastcompany.com/1822516/cafeteria-google-gets-healthy

61. Visual Depiction: Elder, R. and Krishna, A. *"The 'Visual Depiction Effect' in Advertising: Facilitating Embodied Mental Stimulation through Product Orientation"*, 2012 Journal of Consumer Research 988-1003

62. Head and heart: Cian, L., Krishna A., and Schwartz N. *"Positioning Rationality and Emotion: Rationality Is Up and Emotion Is Down"* 2015 Journal of Consumer Research

63. Beauty claims: https://www.ftc.gov/news-events/press-releases/2014/06/loreal-settles-ftc-charges-alleging-deceptive-advertising-anti

64. Beauty claims: http://www.lorealparisusa.com/en/brands/skin-care/revitalift.aspx

65. Beauty claims: https://www.ispot.tv/ad/7fM1/revlon-age-defying-cc-cream-featuring-olivia-wilde

66. Westpac Impulse Saver overview: https://www.youtube.com/watch?v=M9v9HpR4qTU

67. Westpac Impulse Saver results: https://mobiforge.com/news-comment/the-cannes-lions-international-advertising-festival-2011-award-winning-mobile-campaigns-with-case-st

68. Super fund appealing to Now Me: https://www.youtube.com/watch?v=422sJAFXso8

69. Aged images: Hershfield, H., Goldstein, D., Sharpe, W., Fox, J., Yeykelis, L., Carstensen, L. and Bailenson J.*"Increasing saving behavior through age-progressed renderings of the future self"* 2011 Journal of Marketing Research

70. Food on a plane: Gardete, P. *"Social Effects in the In-Flight Marketplace: Characterization and Managerial Implications"* 2015 Journal of Marketing Research. Vol. 52, Issue 3, Pages 360-374

71. Energy use: OPower and Robert Cialdini http://www.slate.com/articles/technology/the_efficient_planet/2013/03/opower_using_smiley_faces_and_peer_pressure_to_save_the_planet.html

72. UK tax: http://hbr.org/2012/10/98-of-hbr-readers-love-this-article/ar/1

73. Facebook usage: http://www.statista.com/statistics/264810/number-of-monthly-active-facebook-users-worldwide/

74. Facebook evolution: http://www.theguardian.com/technology/2007/jul/25/media.newmedia

75. Broccoli: Wansink, B., van Ittersum, K., and Painter, J. *"How descriptive food names bias sensory perceptions in restaurants"* 2004 Food Quality and Preference, 16. No.5

76. Surgery: Jonah Lehrer's *"How We Decide"*

77. Commas: Coulter, K., Choi, P. and Monroe, K. *"Comma N' cents in pricing: The effects of auditory representation encoding on price magnitude perceptions"* 2012 Journal of Consumer Psychology, 22(3), 395–407.

78. Left-digits: Manning, K. and Sprott, D. *"Price Endings, Left-Digit Effects, and Choice."* 2009 Journal of Consumer Research

79. Price ending: Thomas, M. and Morwitz, V. *"Penny Wise and Pound Foolish: The Left Digit Effect in Price Cognition"* 2005 Journal of Consumer Research.

80. Just-below pricing: http://www.sciencedaily.com/releases/2011/09/110906144036.htm

81. eBay rounding: Backus, M., Blake, T., and Tadelis, S. *"Cheap Talk, Round Numbers, and the Economics of Negotiation"* 2015 NBER Working Paper No. 21285

82. Precise numbers: http://www.columbia.edu/~da358/publications/Precise_offers.pdf

83. Font size: Coulter, K., and Coulter R. *"Size Does Matter: The Effects of Magnitude Representation Congruency on Price Perceptions and Purchase Likelihood"* 2005 Journal of Consumer Psychology, 15(1), 64–76

84. Toyota Prius: http://www.academia.edu/239996/Prius_Marketing_Case_Study

85. iPad launch: https://www.youtube.com/watch?v=_KN-5zmvjAo from 1.15:26 mark

86. Up/down: Cian, L., Krishna A., and Schwartz N. *"Positioning Rationality and Emotion: Rationality Is Up and Emotion Is Down"* 2015 Journal of Consumer Research

87. Left/right: Chae, B. and Hoegg, J. *"The Future Looks*

"Right": Effects of the Horizontal Location of Advertising Images on Product Attitude." 2013 Journal of Consumer Research.

88. Menu design: Yang, S., Kimes, S., and Sessarego, M. *"$ or dollars: Effects of menu-price formats on restaurant checks"* 2009, Cornell Hospitality Report, *9*(8), 6-11.

89. Smiley face speeding: http://www.businessinsider.com/can-you-dramatically-change-peoples-behavior-with-a-smiley-face-2011-7/?r=AU&IR=T

90. Smiley face bills: http://www.nytimes.com/2009/01/31/science/earth/31compete.html?scp=1&sq=customers%20green,%20with%20envy&st=cse&_r=0

91. Email likability: Byron, K. and Baldridge, D. *"E-Mail Recipients' Impressions of Senders' Likability"* 2007 International Journal of Business Communication vol. 44 no. 2137-160

92. Retirement plans: Iyengar, S., Huberman, G., and Jiang, W. *"How much choice is too much? Contributions to 401 (k) retirement plans."* 2003 Pension Research Council working paper.

93. Retirement plans: Iyengar, S. and Kamenica, E. *"Choice Proliferation, Simplicity Seeking, and Asset Allocation"* 2010 Journal of Public Economics, Vol. 94, No. 7-8, pp. 530-539

94. Jam study: Iyengar, S. and Lepper, M. *"When Choice is Demotivating: Can One Desire Too Much of a Good Thing?"* 2000 Journal of Personality and Social Psychology, Vol. 79, No. 6, 995-1006

95. Meta-analysis of choice: Scheibehenne, B., Greifeneder R., and Todd, P. *"(When) Does Choice Overload Occur? - a Meta-Analysis"*, 2010 in NA - Advances in Consumer Research Volume 37, Association for Consumer Research, Pages: 499-499

96. Diversification Bias: Salisbury, L. and Feinberg, F. *"Future Preference Uncertainty and Diversification: The Role of Temporal Stochastic Inflation"* 2008 Journal of Consumer Research, Vol. 35 August

97. Decision Quicksand: Sela, A. and Berger, J. *"Decision Quicksand: How Trivial Choices Suck Us In."* 2012 Journal of Consumer Research

98. NY Cabbies: www.fastcodesign.com/1669882/how-touch-screen-buttons-netted-nyc-cabbies-a-cool-144m

99. Center-stage effect: Rodway, P., Schepman, A., and Lambert, J. *"Preferring the One in the Middle: Further Evidence for the Centre-stage Effect"*. 2012 Applied Cognitive Psychology, 26 (2), 215-222

100. 3 points: Carlson, K. and Shu, S. *"When Three Charms But Four Alarms: Identifying the Optimal Number of Claims in Persuasion Settings"* 2014 Journal of Marketing

101. Federer's serve: http://www.tennisabstract.com/blog/ 2011/10/13/us-open-serve-speed-by-player/

102. 2.5x the loss: Daniel Kahneman's *"Thinking Fast and Slow"*

103. 3 points: Carlson, K. and Shu, S. *"When Three Charms But Four Alarms: Identifying the Optimal Number of Claims in Persuasion Settings"* 2014 Journal of Marketing

104. Time to engage: LandofBrand.com cite 0.5 seconds and Marketing Experiments MECLAB cite 7 seconds

105. Car wash: http://www.heraldsun.com.au/leader/east/car-washes-offer-free-cleans-in-24-hour-rain-guarantee/story-fngnvlxu-1226555855993

106. Hyundai Guaranteed Future Value: http:// www.hyundai.com.au/owning/guaranteed-future-value

107. Hyundai Assurance: http://www.thecarconnection.com/ news/1057680_after-26-months-hyundai-assurance-program-gets-its-walking-papers

108. Vaccines: McAuley, I. *"You can see a lot by just looking."* 2008 Centre for Policy Development.

109. Survey question: Based on question in Daniel Kahneman's *"Thinking Fast and Slow"*

110. Jeep TV ad: http://video.news.com.au/v/121917/I-Bought-a-Jeep-advertisement

111. Save More Tomorrow: http://befi.allianzgi.com/en/Topics/ Pages/save-more-tomorrow.aspx

112. Pain of paying: Raghbir P., and Srivastava J. *"Monopoly money: the effect of payment coupling and form on spending behavior."* 2008 J Exp Psychol Appl. Sep;14(3):213-25

113. Returns policy: Janakiraman, N., Syrdal, H. and Freling, R. *"The Effect of Return Policy Leniency on Consumer Purchase and Return Decisions: A Meta-analytic Review"* 2016 Journal of Retailing Volume 92, Issue 2, June 2016, Pages 226–235

114. French café: http://www.thelocal.fr/20131210/photo-of-the-day-french-caf-charges-extra-for-rudeness

115. Buried treasure: http://finance.ninemsn.com.au/pfmanagingmoney/saving/8126677/buried-treasure-dig-up-564m-of-unclaimed-money

116. Cash grab: http://www.news.com.au/finance/money/cash-grab-inactive-bank-accounts-to-be-seized/story-e6frfmcr-1226585867131

117. GLAD: http://www.smartcompany.com.au/marketing/45309-glad-australia-cops-backlash-over-clingwrap-changes-80-metres-of-sheer-frustration.html

118. Polling: http://www.nytimes.com/2015/06/21/opinion/sunday/whats-the-matter-with-polling.html?smprod=nytcore-iphone&smid=nytcore-iphone-share&_r=0

119. Eating habits: http://mobile.abc.net.au/news/2015-06-22/unhealthy-eating-habits-the-new-normal-for-victorians-study/6562924

120. Craft beer: http://qz.com/420295/americans-claim-to-love-craft-beer-but-they-actually-buy-bud-light/

121. Reading choices: http://www.theatlantic.com/business/archive/2014/06/news-kim-kardashian-kanye-west-benghazi/372906/

122. Auctions: Ku. G., Galinsky, A., Murnighan, J. *"Starting low but ending high: a reversal of the anchoring effect in auctions".* 2006 J Pers Soc Psychol.Jun; 90(6):975-86.

123. Rounded numbers: Wadhwa, M. and Zhang, K. *"This Number Just Feels Right: The Impact of Roundedness of Price Numbers on Product Evaluations"* 2015 *Journal of Consumer Research* Vol. 41, No. 5

124. eBay rounding: Backus, M., Blake, T., and Tadelis, S. *"Cheap Talk, Round Numbers, and the Economics of Negotiation"* 2015 NBER Working Paper No. 21285

125. Rounded numbers: Wadhwa, M. and Zhang, K. *"This Number Just Feels Right: The Impact of Roundedness of Price Numbers on Product Evaluations"* 2015 *Journal of Consumer Research* Vol. 41, No. 5 (February 2015), pp. 1172-1185

126. Commas: Coulter, K., Choi, P., and Monroe, K. *"Comma N' cents in pricing: The effects of auditory representation encoding*

on price magnitude perceptions" 2012 Journal of Consumer Psychology, 22(3), 395–407.

127. Font size: Coulter, K. and Coulter R. *"Size Does Matter: The Effects of Magnitude Representation Congruency on Price Perceptions and Purchase Likelihood"* 2005 Journal of Consumer Psychology, 15(1), 64–76

128. Paris hotel: https://www.smartertravel.com/2014/07/22/pay-what-you-want-at-hotels-in-paris/

129. Watching you: Ernest-Jones, M., Nettle, D. and Bateson, M *"Effects of eye images on everyday cooperative behavior: a field experiment."* 2011 Evolution & Human Behavior Volume 32, Issue 3, Pages 172–178

130. PWYW: http://www.gsb.stanford.edu/insights/frank-flynn-pay-what-you-want-pricing-charitable-giving

131. Executive decision making: http://download.predictivetechnologies.com/economist_intelligence_unit_report/

132. Signatures: http://www.smh.com.au/digital-life/digital-life-news/pin-or-pin-visa-mastercard-seek-ban-on-credit-card-signatures-20130723-2qgf4

133. Implanted microchip: http://www.drugfree.org/join-together/implanted-microchips-used-to-pay-bar-tab/

134. Menu design: Yang, S., Kimes, S., and Sessarego, M. *"$ or dollars: Effects of menu-price formats on restaurant checks"* 2009, Cornell Hospitality Report, 9(8), 6-11.

135. Retention stats: ACMA's "Behavioural Economics and Customer Complaints in the Communications industry" May 2011

136. BJ Fogg: My thoughts on the relationship between Motivation and Ability have been inspired by BJ Fogg, with whom I trained a number of years ago. More on his Behaviour Model at www.behaviormodel.org.

137. Woolworths loyalty card: http://www.smh.com.au/business/retail/woolworths-loyalty-program-comes-up-short-20160413-go5axt.html

138. Coles My5: http://www.smartcompany.com.au/finance/economy/28588-coles-abandons-my5-loyalty-program-a-key-lesson-for-smes/

139. Small-area hypothesis: Koo, M., and Fishbach, A. *"The Small-Area Hypothesis: Effects of Progress Monitoring on Goal Adherence."* 2012 Journal of Consumer Research Vol. 39 October

140. Conversion stats: Online Retailing Australia, Forrester Research 2011

141. Time to engage: LandofBrand.com cite 0.5 seconds and Marketing Experiments MECLAB cite 7 seconds

142. Fogg Behaviour Model: http://www.behaviormodel.org/

143. Driving job interview: http://www.nytimes.com/2014/05/04/business/ron-kaplan-of-trex-on-making-judgments-instead-of-decisions.html?_r=0

144. Motivating performance: Kube, S., Maréchal, M. and Puppe, C. *"The Currency of Reciprocity: Gift Exchange in the Workplace."* 2012 American Economic Review, 102(4): 1644-62.

145. Money primes: Vohs K., Mead N. and Goode M. *"The psychological consequences of money."* 2006 Science 17;314(5802)

146. Massage vs money: Cited in "Monetary vs. Non-Monetary Awards: Comparative Studies", by BI Worldwide

147. London School of Economics: http://www.lse.ac.uk/newsAndMedia/news/archives/2009/06/performancepay.aspx

148. Money reduces performance: Ariely, D., Gneezy, U., Loewenstein, G. and Mazar, N. *"Large Stakes and Big Mistakes"* 2009 The Review of Economic Studies Vol. 76, No. 2 (Apr) pp. 451-469

149. Triggertrap: https://medium.com/triggertrap-playbook/fixing-our-company-s-holiday-policy-six-month-update-8343d1e50667

150. BJ Fogg: http://www.behaviormodel.org/

151. Tiny habits: http://tinyhabits.com/

152. Cooking course: https://foodistkitchen.com/

153. Executive decision making: http://download.predictivetechnologies.com/economist_intelligence_unit_report/

154. T.I.C.S. Framework: was developed with a dash of inspiration from Phil Barden's excellent book "Decoded" where he covers tangibility, immediacy and certainty albeit with a different spin, and input on the role of Self Worth from the very clever and highly recommended team at FiftyFive5research, with whom I collaborate.

155. Netflix: http://richardblundell.net/2013/10/netflix/

About the Author

Behavioural Economics for Business is the third book by Behavioural Specialist Bri Williams, following *22 Minutes to a Better Business* (2011) and *The How of Habits* (2014).

Bri was the first in Australia to establish a consultancy specialising in the application of Behavioural Economics to business and personal effectiveness, and since 2011 has worked with a range of large and small businesses on making life easier through behavioural science.

A CPA with a degree in Applied Psychology, Bri writes for Smartcompany and appears regularly as a keynote speaker and panelist. Bri lives in Melbourne but works with clients across Australia and around the world.

More information can be found at www.briwilliams.com.au

Why not get in touch?

Follow Bri on Twitter **@peoplepatterns**
Email Bri via **bri@peoplepatterns.com.au**
Connect with Bri on **LinkedIn**
Call Bri on **0408 392 173**

CPSIA information can be obtained
at www.ICGtesting.com
Printed in the USA
BVOW06s1242090217

475769BV00005B/53/P